Praise for *Product Roadmaps Relaunched*

It's about time someone brought product roadmapping out of the dark ages of waterfall development and made it into the strategic communications tool it should be. McCarthy and team have cracked the code.

Steve Blank, author of *The Startup Owner's Manual*

The theme-driven roadmap is the only way to operate today. By focusing on value rather than features or dates, this book makes product roadmaps useful again.

David Cancel, CEO, Drift

Product roadmaps matter. You can't build a great company unless you have a great strategy and a product roadmap is a way of clearly articulating that strategy. This book makes it clear how to develop the core components of a roadmap, the problem set, the value propositions, and areas of focus for the customer.

Jeffrey Bussgang, General Partner, Flybridge Capital

Product roadmaps bridge the gap between Agile tactics and company strategy. This book is required reading for anyone on my team and I'd recommend it for all software product leaders.

Samuel Clemens, VP of Product Management, InsightSquared

When you follow this book's brilliant advice, a smartly designed roadmap will put your customers directly in the focus of your product strategy. You'll shift from the standard approach of "Look at us and what we can do" to "We understand what you're dealing with and we can help you." Roadmaps will be your company's competitive strategic advantage.

Jared Spool, CEO/Founding Principal of UIE

Product Roadmaps Relaunched

C. Todd Lombardo
Bruce McCarthy
Evan Ryan
Michael Connors

Beijing · Boston · Farnham · Sebastopol · Tokyo

Product Roadmaps Relaunched

by C. Todd Lombardo, Bruce McCarthy, Evan Ryan, Michael Connors

Printed in Canada.

Published by O'Reilly Media, Inc., 1005 Gravenstein Highway North, Sebastopol, CA 95472.

O'Reilly books may be purchased for educational, business, or sales promotional use. Online editions are also available for most titles (*oreilly.com*). For more information, contact our corporate/institutional sales department: (800) 998-9938 or *corporate@oreilly.com*.

Acquisitions Editor: Nick Lombardi
Developmental Editor: Angela Rufino
Production Editor: Melanie Yarbrough
Copyeditor: Rachel Monaghan
Proofreader: Sharon Wilkey
Indexer: Lucie Haskins

Cover Designer: Michael Connors
Interior Designers: Ron Bilodeau and Monica Kamsvaag
Illustrator: Michael Connors
Compositor: Michael Connors

Revision History for the First Edition:

2019-12-20	Ninth release
2020-04-03	Tenth release
2020-09-25	Eleventh release
2021-03-05	Twelfth release
2022-01-14	Thirteenth release

See *http://oreilly.com/catalog/errata.csp?isbn=0636920055983* for release details.

978-1-491-97172-7

[TI]

Contents

"No roadmap survives contact with reality."

It's a saying that has flourished in product management circles for years—for all the wrong reasons.

Roadmaps get a lot of flak. They are often blamed for unrealistic deadlines and death marches. For missing market opportunities, and for building features that are out-of-date before any code is even written.

When I began my career as a product manager, a roadmap was commonly known as a feature-by-feature wish list, outlining releases and delivery dates stretching as far out into the future as the spreadsheet could handle. My own roadmap was a work of art—an all-singing, all-dancing dynamic spreadsheet that certainly pleased the bosses...but terrified the developers and let me down every quarter when it had to be tediously updated to match with all the things we weren't able to deliver.

I even went so far as to neatly package up this spreadsheet and release it into the wild for others to download. At the time, I thought I was being helpful, but it just fueled the trend for beautiful, but ultimately treacherous, roadmap formats.

And these old artifacts are still everywhere: do a Google image search for *Product Roadmap* and you'll see what I mean.

But an old-school roadmap doesn't fit with modern software development. And a modern roadmap isn't *meant* to survive contact with reality.

Just as your first prototypes and MVPs are likely to get trashed in feedback sessions with your early customers, your roadmap is meant to change and adapt as you learn more.

Your product roadmap is the prototype for your strategy.

It's your key to vision alignment. It's your ever-adaptable communication aid, the one thing your team can coalesce around and use as a North Star guiding light.

In this book, Bruce, C. Todd, Evan, and Michael finally set the record straight. Roadmaps are a powerful communication tool that benefit not just the product people and their immediate team, but the entire company and how it communicates.

The authors have unburdened the rest of us by digging out the absolute best practices from product-centric companies around the world and lining them up in a way that'll empower you, the product person, to create and maintain a roadmap that will propel you forward instead of hold you back.

It's the first book to hold up the product roadmap as not just a document, but a leadership tool.

And it couldn't come at a better time. As cofounder of Mind the Product and the ProductTank events around the world, I see how roadmaps are being created, communicated, and shared.

Time and time again, I see product teams who are being held back by outdated roadmapping practices.

Much of my time is spent on trying to rid the world of bad road maps—and it's not just me. As Marty Cagan once said to me, "At least 90% of the roadmaps I see are squarely in the 'bad' category."

Now Bruce, C. Todd, Evan, and Michael are doing something about it, and this book is a giant leap forward in fixing the problem. I only wish it had existed years ago, when it could have saved me from many of the roadmap struggles I went through! Perhaps I would have thought better of releasing that well-meaning but ill-advised roadmap template.

Just as lean/agile facilitated a step-change in how we iterate and deliver, this relaunched roadmap paves the way to change how we discover opportunities, communicate about them, and build products that solve real problems.

It's time for a relaunch, to move into a new way of roadmapping, and this book is it.

*—**Janna Bastow**,*
Cofounder/CEO of ProdPad and
cofounder of Mind the Product
Brighton, UK—July 2017

Dear Roadmap

"Why are you writing a book about product roadmaps? Does anyone even do those anymore?"

Each of us has been asked questions along these lines repeatedly over the last few months. We've also had the opposite reaction: "We're redoing our roadmapping process right now. It's so broken. When is your book coming out? Can I get a sneak preview?" At the same time that many are calling roadmaps old-fashioned, we're seeing more and more people sign up for our roadmapping workshops.

Roadmaps were once required for any technology-related effort. They communicated specific deliverables and deadlines, and generally provided a comforting sense that everything was well planned and on track.

In the past decade, though, product roadmaps have become controversial. People seek the perfect roadmapping process and frequently end up disappointed. Many have actually abandoned the process in frustration, but retain this nagging sense that they are missing the strategic big picture.

As you read in the "Dear Roadmap" letters, product people are breaking up with their roadmapping process because it's no longer delivering on its promise.

Dear Roadmap,

I've been putting in so much energy to get this relationship working, but it feels like I only give and never get any value back from you!

* You are always out of date
* There is no way to get all the information in and keep it looking nice and readable
* You are all about solutions and not about the needs and the problems
* You are never good enough for all the different stakeholders.

THIS IS IT!

I'M GOING BACK TO MS PROJECT!

Dear Roadmap,
   You have deceived me....
You lead me down a path
of lies, painting a picture
of our future together
— all the wonderful things
we'd create together —
the history we'd write —
that was all lies!
   I gave you everything
you asked for -- support,
encouragement, forgiveness
when you failed, even
money -- and still you
haven't been true....

Dear Roadmap,

No one trusts you... STILL? You
have evolved over and over again
and have made great
progress when used as a
communication tool however
you are not shiny enough
to keep stakeholders
engaged. People still just
want a list with dates/features.
How can we change the
way people look at you?
I believe you can be great one
day.
      — Meghan

DEAR J. ROADMAP,

    I AM LEAVING YOU BECAUSE I CAN'T TRUST YOU. YOU PROMISE THAT IF I FOLLOW YOU, I WILL BECOME HEALTHY, WEALTHY & WISE. INSTEAD, I'VE BECOME FAT, DUMB & UNHAPPY.

    YOU PAINT A BRIGHT FUTURE. BUT YOU NEVER GET US THERE.

                 LOVE, BOB

Dear Johnny Roadmap.
I'm done. It's not working.
You are hard to talk to,
Cumbersome to communicate
with, I never know exactly
where we stand. My
friends never agree with
you and we never agree
on what's most important
+ what come next.
      Hasta la vista
        Johnny

They want a document that:

- Puts the organization's plans in a strategic, value-oriented context
- Is based on market and user research rather than guess-work and opinion
- Gets customers excited about their product direction
- Rallies their organization around a single set of priorities
- Embraces learning and evolving as part of a successful product development process
- Doesn't require a wasteful process of up-front design and estimation

Perhaps the traditional product roadmap was once useful, when the goal (sell more units) was obvious, the pace of change was slower, and Moore's law created a sense of inevitable and steady progress in the semiconductor industry of the 80s and 90s.

If this was ever true, though, it certainly has changed. It seems technology projects seldom, if ever, go according to plan. How many target ship dates have you actually hit? Exactly. Dates slip. Priorities change. Features are cut. Business models change. Companies "pivot." Worse, as an industry, we've learned that those efforts that do go precisely to plan seldom deliver the value expected from the things the roadmap has outlined.

David Cancel, CEO of Drift and former head of product for HubSpot, summed up these frustrations well when he explained why he no longer puts together a traditional roadmap: "Either I'm going to disappoint you by giving you exactly what

we thought six months ahead of time was the best solution when it's not, or by changing course and having lied to you."

Things have changed and product roadmaps haven't caught up. They haven't adapted to a world of lean and agile (some would even say post-agile) organizations. But there is still a need (even a hunger) for the vision, direction, and rallying cry that a good roadmap provides. To meet this need, roadmaps need a refresh—a relaunch, so to speak.

Fortunately, there is a new generation of product people developing a new breed of product roadmap. We're seeing it come together in bits and pieces from sources as far apart as enterprise software, electronic components, consumer apps, business services, and even medicine.

We've assembled these best practices into a flexible framework that provides a powerful toolset for product people, and represents a new paradigm in product roadmapping.

Marty Cagan, founder of Silicon Valley Product Group and author of *Inspired: How to Create Products Customers Love* (SVPG Press), describes this new paradigm as follows: "It's all about solving problems, not implementing features. Conventional product roadmaps are all about output. Strong teams know it's not only about implementing a solution; they must ensure that solution actually solves the underlying problem. It's about results."

Intrigued?

Read on and join the relaunch of product roadmapping.

Who Is This Book For?

This book is written for product people. If you're wondering if that's you, we're referring to the individual or individuals responsible for developing, prioritizing, and rallying support for the development of a product or service. This role has been compared to "a mini CEO," but we think that overstates the level of control most product people have.

We prefer the analogy of the executive chef, the person who brings together kitchen staff, menu, and purchasing—and even trains the front-of-house staff—all in order to bring in customers, satisfy their hunger, and make money for the business. It is not enough for an executive chef to simply distribute the work, but each team member must understand whom they are serving, and why they are doing things a certain way, so as to create a seamless experience for the customer.

In many organizations (and particularly in technology organizations), this responsibility carries the title of product manager, product director, or product owner. Depending on the nature of your business and structure of your team, however, these duties may be handled by a myriad of other roles and functions, including project manager, development manager, engineering manager, technical lead, operations manager, program manager, user experience designer, customer success, quality assurance, and many more. In today's fast-moving business environment, responsibilities and titles can change as frequently as the technologies we work with.

We wrote this book to be accessible to anyone involved in product, regardless of title. If your job includes strategizing about where your product is going, contributing to alignment around a shared vision, or developing a plan to execute, then we hope this book will be relevant, enlightening, and useful to you.

In addition, we want this book to be useful for product people of all experience levels. Whether you're a product "newbie," a seasoned veteran, or a senior leader responsible for a range of products (or a team of product people), we believe the approach we describe here will help you and your team communicate product direction effectively.

Maybe you had never heard of product roadmapping before you came across this book. That's OK! (Welcome aboard, we have life jackets.) If you're new to product development or new to the concept of roadmapping, we've designed this book to be a helpful introduction.

Or maybe you have a product roadmapping process but have realized it's flawed. Maybe what you thought was a product roadmap was actually a business plan, a marketing plan, or a project plan.

Recognizing that you don't have a working product roadmapping process is actually a great place to be. This means you can wipe the slate clean and start fresh.

How to Use This Book

Product roadmapping isn't a destination; rather, it's a journey, marked by a collection of actions that help define how to deliver the highest possible value to the customer. The following list identifies the key principles we've found are crucial to a successful product roadmap. You may already have some of these in place, and each company, product, and set of stakeholders is different, so we'll talk about how you can mix and match based on your needs and the readiness of your organization.

- Gather inputs (Chapter 3)

- Establish the product vision (Chapter 4)

- Uncover customer needs (Chapter 5)

- Dive deeper into needs and solutions (Chapter 6)

- Master the art and science of prioritization (Chapter 7)

- Achieve buy-in and alignment (Chapter 8)

- Present and share (Chapter 9)

- Keep it fresh (Chapter 10)

We've organized the core of this book in the order of these tasks; however, our research has found that there's no "right" order. In addition, Chapter 1 makes the case for a new approach to product roadmapping, Chapter 2 provides an overview of the core components, and Chapter 11 summarizes the entire process.

Roadmapping is not something most product people do every day. Like good cuisine, it is seasonal. So, like your favorite cookbook, this book was designed as a reference you can keep handy to refresh your memory on the intricacies, options, and pitfalls associated with each step along the way.

Why Listen to Us?

As long-time product people ourselves, we've spent decades exploring and using different approaches to product roadmapping. Every organization we've worked for or with has had slightly different needs, and our approaches have varied with them. Upon reflecting on these experiences and comparing approaches, we developed this common framework that we believe any product person can benefit from.

C. Todd Lombardo

Having made all the mistakes one makes as a product manager, C. Todd Lombardo spent over seven years in product at a variety of organizations from startup to enterprise. Trained in science, design, and business, he not only has too many degrees, he loves combining the approach of all three disciplines in his endeavors. He's the Head of Product & Experience at Boston-based Workbar, an Adjunct Professor at IE Business School in Madrid, and coauthor of the first book on Design Sprints, appropriately titled *Design Sprint* (O'Reilly).

Bruce McCarthy

As a young man, Bruce used LEGOs to obtain food and attract a mate. Product is probably encoded somewhere in his DNA.

His is currently president of the Boston Product Management Association (BPMA) and CEO of UpUp Labs.

For some years now, Bruce has been speaking to standing room–only crowds about product roadmapping and strategic prioritization at ProductCamps and other conferences around the world.

He and his team help organizations get more from their investments in product development, working with companies such as Vistaprint, Localytics, Zipcar, Johnson & Johnson, and Huawei, providing coaching, mentoring, and tools such as Awesomeness, a solution for measurably enhancing team effectiveness.

Evan Ryan

To build is to learn. For Evan, creating products and services is about solving mission-critical problems to make the world a better place, but just as important, a chance to learn and explore. Product work provides him with an outlet for his insatiable curiosity.

Evan is an experienced product leader and entrepreneur who has brought dozens of products from concept to market for both consumer and enterprise audiences. He specializes in understanding ecosystems and extracting user insights to guide strategy and drive innovation. As a founder, his companies have served a diverse variety of organizations, from startups, to nonprofits, to Fortune 500 companies, including Apple, Deloitte, Chevron, Sonos, Stanford University, and others.

Evan extends his knowledge and learning to others through speaking engagements, custom workshops, and as an adjunct professor who teaches classes on design and entrepreneurship. This is his first book for O'Reilly Media, but the writing bug is now firmly embedded.

Michael Connors

Michael has spent his career as a designer of all kinds of digital and print deliverables. He was trained as a fine artist and has an MFA in Painting. Currently, he's the Creative Director at Fresh Tilled Soil, a Boston-based UX/UI design firm, where he works on digital products for major brands, startups, and everything in between. He's also an Adjunct Professor at IE Business School in Madrid and has been an adjunct design instructor at other institutions of higher ed for many years. He lives in Northampton, Massachusetts where he enjoys his front porch every chance he gets.

Acknowledgments

C. Todd would like to thank all the product teams we interviewed on the journey to this book; Faye Boeckman and John Linnan—you were two of my first product mentors, and your wisdom has guided me for years after we worked together; Bruce and Evan for agreeing to come on this book-writing journey with me; MC for bringing the design awesomesauce and framing the content in such a professorial manner; the amazing team at Mind the Product for connecting us with just about any product person on the planet; the team at Fresh Tilled Soil for being patient with Evan and I while we pursued this crazy roadmapping thing; and my colleagues at Workbar who inspire me to make the best damn products I've ever made. It goes without saying that the team at O'Reilly was supportive and helpful in helping us bring this concept to life, and I'm so grateful for the opportunity to publish this book with you.

Bruce would like to thank Anthony Accardi for reminding us to focus on the "why" of what's on the roadmap; Ben Foster for making it clear why alignment is at least as important as strategy; Bill Allen for describing the ideal practice of shuttle diplomacy; Bob Levy for describing how customers can influence the roadmap constructively; Jeff Bussgang for calling bullshit on roadmap unbelievers; Emily Tyson for describing the use of confidence in a roadmap; Matt Peopsel for articulating the proper use of themes; Steve Blank for articulating the weaknesses in the traditional roadmap; Bryan Dunn for the nine-hour roadmap and using the roadmap to say no; David Cancel for being his contrarian self; Frank Capria for insights on how much to share with customers and sales; Alex Kohlhofer for cautioning against recency bias; Andrea Blades for letting him experiment on her team; Gillian Daniel for validating so much of our framework; Janna Bastow for highlighting the differences between public and internal roadmaps; Jim Kogler for describing the organic process of customer feedback; Jim Semick for reminding us of the value of fuzziness in planning; Jim Garretson for highlighting the differences between buyer and user priorities; John Mansour for crisply describing the difference between a roadmap and a release plan; Joseph Gracia for describing the value of conversation with stakeholders; Julia Austin for reminding us to balance strategic direction with customer feedback; Matt Morasky for thoughts on small increments; Michael Salerno for bringing us back to the problem statement; Nate Archer for recognizing roadmapping as an emergent behavior of effective teams; Nils Davis for describing the relationship between the roadmap and the detail hidden beneath; Roger Cauvin for explaining how he uses roadmaps to focus the team on a product vision; Rose Grabowski for beautifully describing the roadmap as a sales document; Saeed Kahn for revealing how creating a roadmap improves his product strategy; Samuel Clemens for describing the roadmap itself as his product; Sarela Bliman-Cohen for tying themes to market segments; Sherif Mansour for the concepts of persona-driven, goal-driven, and vision-driven roadmaps; Teresa Torres for her amazing Opportunity Solution tree visualization; Torrance Robinson for articulating how to use roadmaps to keep yourself honest; and Vanessa Ferranto for highlighting the difference between a problem and a hypothesis.

Thanks are due also to Bruce's colleagues and friends at the Boston Product Management Association (BPMA) for their unfailing support. And to all of the reviewers who gave positive and constructive feedback throughout the book. Bruce would especially like to thank Keith Hopper for his relentless and detailed candor. The book is much better for all of your attention.

Bruce would also like to thank C. Todd for persuading (OK, arm-twisting) him to be part of this effort; Andrew Shepard and Steve Robins for egging him on; his daughter, Amanda McCarthy, for being the world's fastest (and most accurate) copy editor and quote wrangler; Sandra Ocasio for patiently scheduling and rescheduling about a million Skype interviews; Angela Rufino for the patience of Job (and like Job, for never giving up); and the love of his life, Christine Moran McCarthy, for understanding he needed to do this.

Evan would like to thank his coauthors for enduring his endless search for answers with grace and humor and for the constant willingness to weather new depths of exploration (even after exhaustion set in). For the great team of editors and advisors at O'Reilly, thank you for the encouragement to write the book and the flexibility needed to work through countless revisions. To his fellow product leaders, those he knows well and those he doesn't know yet, thank you for the constant inspiration. His contributions to this book are supported by the expertise and encouragement of his peers in the product space. Your willingness to be interviewed and answer hard questions provided the canvas on which we could work. To the friends, family members, investors, advisors, and mentors that supported him at every step in his entrepreneurial wanderings, a deep, deep thank you. Without your guidance and generosity, he would not be where he is today, and writing a book like this would be a distant goal. Thank you as well to his FTS colleagues for being willing guinea pigs on all things roadmap, and to the leadership for clearing a path and supporting this project. To his close friends, a deep thank you for keeping him sane. To his immediate family—mom, dad, Casey, and Kellie—thank you for your endless confidence and support. Finally, to his wife, Jenna, thank you for your love and unquestioning faith. You inspire me to keep striving.

Michael would like to thank his coauthors for many things, but first for inviting him to be a part of this book. Also in tirelessly defining and refining the book's core concepts and structure, their willingness to share and debate ideas openly and freely, and their commitment to create something useful; the entire O'Reilly team, but especially Melanie and Angela (rockstars); his friends, colleagues, collaborators, students, advisors, clients (many of whom are also the former) on the project teams that have helped him hone his craft; his parents, Bob and Ellie; his siblings for keeping him honest and for challenging everything (and he means everything) all these years; the countless, largely anonymous "blue-collar" designers, creatives, and craftspeople that have created, and still create the rich visual and experiential culture from which we all benefit.

Chapter 1

Relaunching Roadmaps

What you'll learn in this chapter

A few definitions, including:

- Product
- Customer
- Stakeholder

Where product roadmaps came from

Requirements for a roadmap relaunch

What is a product roadmap?

Chapter 1

Relaunching Roadmaps

Properly done, a product roadmap can steer your entire organization toward delivering on the company strategy.

It is your vision for how your products will help achieve your organization's strategic goals. A good roadmap inspires buy-in and over-delivery from your entire organization.

It's easy to think of a roadmap as a fixed and detailed plan—etched in stone almost—and this is where product people often find frustration sets in. A traditional roadmap is not flexible enough for the lean and agile methods many teams have adopted, and it is often light on the strategic context necessary for teams to understand the overall vision. This is why a re-launch is necessary.

A good roadmap is not so much a project plan as *a strategic communication tool, a statement of intent and direction*. In this chapter, we describe the key requirements for relaunching roadmaps as effective treasure maps for the value you'll deliver to your customer and your organization. Get out your spyglass and compass, and let's get started.

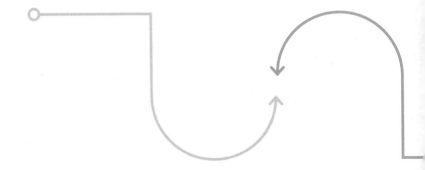

What Is a Product Roadmap?

Product
Vision

In our view, a product roadmap describes how you intend to achieve your product vision.

It focuses on the value you propose to deliver to your customer and your organization in order to rally support and coordinate effort among stakeholders.

It's that simple. And that simplicity is critical to success. Remember, however, that simple does not always equal easy.

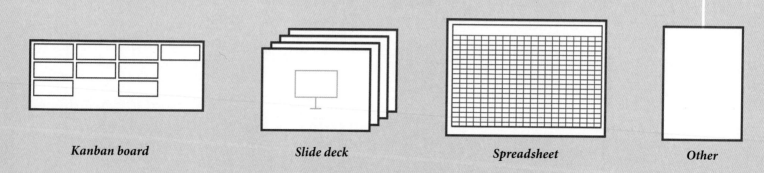

Kanban board	**Slide deck**	**Spreadsheet**	**Other**

FIGURE 1-1. *Product roadmaps can take many forms, and aren't necessarily a single artifact or document. In fact, it's really not about creating artifacts at all—it's about creating a shared understanding of where you're going and why.*

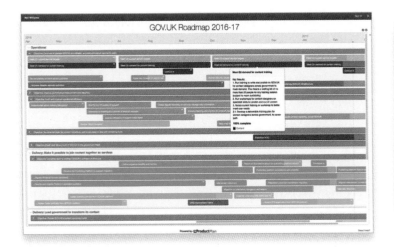

FIGURE 1-2. *Roadmap examples in different shapes and sizes, from a single page to a multipage document*

Key Terms and How We're Using Them

Product

Before we define a product roadmap in detail, let's first describe what we mean by a *product*. A product is how you deliver value to your organization's customers. We usually think of a product as an artifact, like a smartphone or a toaster, but our broader definition includes services like pizza delivery, a Netflix subscription, or even an experience like a Broadway play. To keep it simple, throughout this book we'll refer to whatever you deliver to your customers as your "product."

Stakeholder

We use the term *stakeholder* to refer to all the internal and external colleagues and partners who are involved with the product being developed, marketed, sold, and serviced. Internally this could range from sales, marketing, user experience, engineering, research, finance, and even human resources; externally this could imply partners such as suppliers, technology partners, vendors, resellers, or brokers.

Customer

We use the term *customer* to refer to the recipient of the value your product provides, so let's define that as well. Within that term, we include the buyer and the user of your product. (We'll talk more about the differences in Chapter 3.) In many consumer products, the buyer and the user are the same person. I buy a cup of coffee and I drink it to help me wake up and focus (and because I like the taste). You buy a watch and you strap it on each morning to help keep you on schedule.

However, I might buy a watch for you as a present, separating the role of buyer from that of user. This split is very common in business, where someone in the IT department selects and buys the computers, phones, and other equipment and software that all of the employees use. We'll call out the difference when important; otherwise, we will refer to both buyer and user as the "customer."

It's also worth noting that customers may receive value without payment, per se. Some products are free or supported by advertising, like Gmail or broadcast TV. And some products are created and used within the same organization, for example a corporate intranet where employees can learn about benefit programs and company events.

Where Did Product Roadmaps Come From?

It all starts with the bicycle. In the 1890s, bicycles were a key form of transportation within cities, and some of the first roadmaps were created to show how to bike from one part of New York City to another. With the rise of the automobile, travel between cities becomes more common, and flourishing organizations like the American Automobile Association (AAA) provided printed roadmap directions for travelers. Even today, we are still using roadmaps in electronic form, like Waze and GPS navigation, to direct us to our destinations.

In the 1980s, Motorola began using the term *roadmap* to align technology and product development. Technology roadmaps became widely accepted in the 1990s across the semiconductor industry and were eventually adopted by many other technology-driven organizations, including Microsoft, Google, and Oracle. These roadmaps were created to inform stakeholders of when major upgrades were coming so they could plan their purchases many months in advance. This is still important when you are manufacturing the chips for millions of electronic devices that themselves have long manufacturing lead times. Planning was and continues to be essential in such businesses.

The ever-increasing pace of change in technology, however, coupled with adoption of lean and agile practices that leverage rapid release cycles, learning, and data-driven product decisions, has made the traditional roadmap an unwieldy instrument. Dates slip, technologies become obsolete, priorities shift, customer preferences evolve, the competition gains ground…. As a result, product people increasingly have found themselves caught between breaking promises and staying the course on a plan made months ago that seems increasingly out of touch.

The mismatch between traditional roadmaps and the reality of most product development efforts has gotten bad enough that many product teams have abandoned the practice altogether or restricted access to the roadmap to a few trusted team members.

Few are satisfied with this state of affairs, however. Agile and lean methods have not filled the strategy gap created when roadmaps are left behind. If anything, agile teams complain they spend so much time focused on the next few weeks that they lose sight of the reasons they are doing all this work.

So let's define what it would take to make a good roadmap today.

Requirements for a Roadmap Relaunch

As we outlined in the preface, the product people we've talked to are looking for certain things from a roadmap.

A product roadmap should:

- Put the organization's plans in a strategic context

- Focus on delivering value to customers and the organization

- Embrace learning as part of a successful product development process

- Rally the organization around a single set of priorities

- Get customers excited about the product's direction

At the same time, a product roadmap should not:

- Make promises product teams aren't confident they will deliver on

- Require a wasteful process of up-front design and estimation

- Be conflated with a project plan or a release plan (we cannot stress this enough)

Let's take a closer look at each of these requirements, what problem each is intended to solve, and a little about how a relaunch of roadmapping can solve it. We'll also guide you to chapters that explore each of these concepts in more detail along the way.

A Roadmap Should Put the Organization's Plans in a Strategic Context

Problem: Nobody understands why things are on the roadmap

The traditional roadmap was so focused on deliverables that it often left out the critical context of *why* the organization is focused on these specific things at all. Product people spend enormous amounts of time sifting through market data and customer input; they prioritize, estimate, design, architect, and schedule, but then too often forget to clearly explain their thinking to the people involved in execution.

This is a problem within the product development team itself because without a sense of the big picture, the many decisions engineers, designers, and production people must make on their own are not united by a common vision. The same lack of vision hampers efforts to coordinate with other departments such as marketing, sales, finance, and support.

The roadmap is a critical—and frequently missed—opportunity to articulate why you are doing this product, why it's important, and why the things on it are absolutely vital to success.

Symptoms of this particular problem include:

- Your product doesn't get the funding, shelf space, or marketing support it needs.

- You get lots of questions about the details (features, dates) on your roadmap.

- You get lots of ideas for things to add to the roadmap that don't fit with your vision (the one you haven't clearly articulated).

"We suffer from 'shiny object' syndrome."

"No one knows what our end goal should be."

Solution: Tie the roadmap to a compelling vision of the future

"This is our vision of why we're here and what we're trying to accomplish for clients, and here's the roadmap that's going to help us progressively get there."

—Matt Poepsel, Vice President, Product Development,
The Predictive Index

Before you get into the details of what you and your team are working on, take a moment to explain the big picture. Why are you doing this product in the first place? What will it mean if you are successful—to the customer, to the company, to the world?

Maybe your company has a mission statement, a vision, or a purpose. A good place to start in defining your product vision is to link it to your organization's reason for being.

Then, if everything on your roadmap is clearly there to support that mission, the "why" becomes much more evident. Conversations change from "Why are we doing that?" to "Would decision A or B help us achieve our vision sooner?" Steve Blank, author of The Startup Owner's Manual, reminds us to start with the mission, strategic intent and only then devise the plan from there. "Let's take Airbnb. The mission is, 'We want to change how people view temporary housing. Okay. What's our goal? We want to have 5 million users, 16 million places to rent, how do we do this? We need to deliver software that allows people to do this. OK, what kind of features do we need?'"

Your product roadmap should slot right in between your company vision and your more detailed development, release, and operational plans.

Chapter 4 goes into much more detail on creating a product vision and measurable goals.

A Roadmap Should Focus on Delivering Value to Customers and the Organization

Problem: You are shipping a lot but not making progress

"A lot of people think a feature release schedule and roadmap are synonymous, right? You've probably heard that a hundred times. In fact, if you look at any of the software programs I've seen out there for product roadmapping, they're a graphical version of this feature x on with a delivery date. In my mind, a roadmap is a series of statements that communicate WHAT you'll help customers accomplish and WHY those goals are important to their success."

—John Mansour, Managing Partner, Proficientz

The traditional product roadmap is really more of a project plan focused on efficient use of resources, maximizing throughput, and hitting dates. Many highly detailed roadmaps, however, entirely leave out discussion of what is expected as a *result* of all this effort.

Many teams have begun measuring the actual effect of additions or changes to their product on customer behavior and business results, but this is usually absent from the roadmap. The only criteria left for management to judge success of product development efforts, then, is whether the team shipped on time—*but*

does being on schedule make any difference if you have no effect on customer behavior or business results?

Symptoms of this particular problem include:

- Releases happen on time but don't change any of your business KPIs (key performance indicators).

- Implementing customer requests doesn't increase customer satisfaction.

- Features meet the specs without solving the problem for the customer.

"I have no insight into how my team's work affects the bottom line."

"I never really talk directly to our customers."

Solution: Focus the roadmap on delivering value

After you've described the product vision and what everyone's there to accomplish, the next level down in detail should not be a laundry list of features, functions, and fixes with dates. Instead—even if you are pretty certain about some of the specifics—we recommend starting with the chunks of value you intend to deliver that will build up over time to accomplish your vision.

Often this is a set of high-level customer needs, problems, or jobs to be done, which we call *themes*. To borrow an example from the next chapter, the most basic job a garden hose needs to do is to transport water from the spigot to the garden. All hoses do that well enough, but many present the customer with problems like kinks and leaks that prevent all the water from reaching its destination. The garden hose product roadmap might, then, include a statement of the customer's need for (i.e., a theme of) "indestructibility."

This makes the goal of the next version, variation, or feature of the product very clear to all stakeholders, including the people responsible for designing and manufacturing it. David Cancel, CEO of Drift, says, "We wanted as much autonomy down at the engineering and product team level as possible. Of course, there were some of what we call guardrails and goalposts. Within those guardrails, they could decide what that product looked like or how we were going to go to market."

Critically for the roadmap, these guardrails also provide a means of judging when you are done that is separate from the due dates. To return to our earlier example, you are done when you have an indestructible hose you can manufacture and sell at a profit.

Ben Foster, an advisor to product-driven startups, expands on the idea that uncovering themes to deliver value is more important than simply hitting deadlines: "I prefer to keep dates as vague as possible in order to maintain flexibility. If I don't have sufficient confidence an item on the roadmap will be delivered by a specific date then, I don't want to commit to it. The roadmap should clarify plans, but without providing false precision that someone else might be banking on."

In Chapter 5, we'll delve further into what themes are and how to develop them for your roadmap.

► A Roadmap Should Embrace Learning

Problem: Executives and customers demand commitments

"I think the biggest challenge a roadmap has is that it's sort of your expectation of how your production is going to happen. If the salesperson gets a little bit aggressive with it because they think it's going to help them win a deal, I think that's the classic mistake. It becomes a commitment, and if something changes in your business and it's not in the best interest of the company to go down that path, that's when it blows up in your face."

—Matt Poepsel, Vice President, Product Development,
The Predictive Index

These high-level themes and broad date ranges we describe are fine, you might be thinking, but what happens when the customer says they won't sign the big contract without a commitment to a specific feature this year? Or the CEO feels that extracting blood oaths is the way to ensure everyone is working hard enough?

Again, the traditional roadmap tries so hard to predict an unpredictable future that it invites these kinds of conversations. It would be much better to have a conversation about value, wouldn't it? About goals? About why the features the customer is demanding are important and what problems are driving their thinking and priorities?

If you've done a good job articulating the value you intend to deliver, the details of how you will deliver it are certainly less important. In fact, they are not just a distraction, they're actually an impediment to delivering the most value. By committing too early to a single solution to a problem, you are constraining your options and stifling your team's creativity.

Symptoms of this particular problem include:

- Salespeople write commitments into contracts to win a deal.

- Customers extract promises before they will sign.

- Executives feel that date commitments are the only way to get results.

"We have a lot of data but we don't know how to use it."

"Our process is broken but we avoid fixing it."

"I have no idea how other teams or other companies roadmap."

Solution: Commit to outcomes rather than output

When a customer (or a CEO, or really any stakeholder) asks about whether a particular feature or design or other detail will be part of the solution, rather than answer the question, experienced product people have learned to turn it around. They ask "Why?" Why is that feature important to you? What is it about that date? The smartest product people are trying to understand what problem that stakeholder is trying to solve. This helps them understand their customers' needs better, of course, but it also raises the level of discussion.

With an understanding of the real goal, a product person can then ask the customer, "If I commit to solving this problem for you the best way I can, then do we have a deal?" Or, as Drift's David Cancel suggests, "Rather than try to predict the future, why don't I invite you into our process? If you are a key strategic customer, then when we get close to a possible solution for the thing that is of concern to you, we'll bring you into a design review and let you give us feedback about whether it meets your needs."

When customers and other stakeholders make these demands, it's because they don't know how else to influence product direction. And some of them really do have hard dates or specs that must be met; for example, to make a production schedule or meet regulatory standards. If you can create a relationship of trust, though, by being really honest about what you know and what you don't, customers will understand when you have to change directions or priorities on the roadmap.

Alex Kohlhofer, Director of Product for UserVoice, says, "Prospects do sometimes ask for things in the contract, but we've never done it. We might learn things that would trump that request in importance. We sometimes lose deals based on customer asks we cannot guarantee, but we have lots of customers, and I need to do what's best for most of them, not just a few of them."

Matt Poepsel adds that the customer must "be a responsible consumer of the roadmap to understand that things that are far out in that roadmap, you just can't take them as strictly, exactly what's going to happen. These aren't commitments so much as they're intentions."

Chapter 9 describes ways to decide how frequently to update your roadmap and how to communicate change.

► A Roadmap Should Rally the Organization Around a Single Set of Priorities

Problem: Marketing and sales are not selling what you are making

"I think that in recent years, it's become generally recognized that having the right strategy only matters if there's total alignment around it. When marketing is telling one story, sales is selling something different, and engineering is building something different still, then product management's strategy is hollow and irrelevant. The roadmap must align all the stakeholders around a common product plan."

—Ben Foster, advisor to product-driven startups

Foster's point reiterates the starring role your product vision must play in your roadmap, and how important it is to explain the value of each component on it to the customer and to the organization.

But even if you've done a good job with all of that, the challenge you'll face next is setting priorities. The fact is, there are just too many good ideas for any team—of any size—to implement. You can't do everything at once, so you have to pick and choose.

Getting alignment on priorities is not easy, but it's critical to execution. Organizations that don't align well around the roadmap miss market opportunities because it takes months for marketing and sales to catch up to what the product team is putting out there. In some organizations, products perform poorly because the marketing and sales teams never had the opportunity to buy in and achieve this alignment.

Symptoms of this particular problem include:

- Marketing doesn't know how to explain your product to the market.

- Sales continues selling last year's products.

- You receive lots of ideas for the roadmap, none of which make the cut.

"What are our other product teams doing?"

"We see the same roadmap items again and again."

Solution: Align everyone around common goals and priorities

As Carol Meyers, CMO of Rapid7, puts it, "At some point, you need to start talking with the sales force about, 'Hey, we think we're going to be bringing this new product to market. What's the best way to go to market? Can our current reps sell it, or should we have specialized reps? How do we get everybody trained up to understand the customer's problem and the solution we're bringing to market?'"

The best way we've found to rally these people is to involve them in the decisions that will affect them. This requires that you share some of your thinking early, before the relevant parts of the roadmap are really concrete, to get their input. Emily Tyson, VP Product at NaviHealth, says: "Every product manager actually has their own stakeholder advisory group—cross-functional representatives that they work with to get input on: What are priorities for sales? What are priorities from the clinical team?

What does security need in the roadmap? The product team is very much responsible for taking all of the different inputs and saying, 'This is it.'"

Chapter 7 details a number of techniques for setting priorities based on your guiding principles.

Chapter 8 then goes on to explain in detail how to gain that critical buy-in and alignment from your stakeholders.

A Roadmap Should Get Customers Excited About the Product Direction

Problem: Customers aren't excited about your new features

"How do product teams really know the right thing to build? Many products aren't successful because teams haven't done enough problem discovery and validation with customers. Those processes need to be a part of a product team's culture."

—Jim Semick, Founder, ProductPlan

Just hitting your target dates and intended feature releases is no guarantee of market acceptance nor of business success. A healthy amount of experimentation can help establish what needs to be built and the metrics against which products will be measured prior to building and shipping. A roadmap has been called a prototype of your strategy, and allowing customers to view your roadmap allows them to offer feedback on and buy into your direction.

Sharing a roadmap with customers is scary for many product people. They naturally worry that anything they say will be held against them in the future if things change (and they always do). More courageously, Jim Kogler, VP of products at VT MAK, sees the advantage of sharing: "I use the roadmap as a lubricant for effective communication in front of a customer." Experienced practitioners differ on this point, but more often than not

the benefits of sharing early and often with customers outweigh the risks. The trick is in framing the conversation correctly.

Symptoms of this particular problem include:

- Customers don't use the new features you've worked so hard on.

- Sales plateau (or decline) despite improvements and updates.

- A customer confronts you with a copy of last year's roadmap and accuses you of breaking your promises (shiver).

"We don't expose new ideas to customers."

"We don't validate needs before building things."

Solution: Use the roadmap to reality-check your direction with customers

"A roadmap is a two-way communication device. When a customer sees a roadmap, when they see what I'm showing them, we start a dialog about business pain and priorities. They tell me, 'Oh, that's going to solve a problem for me.'"

—Michael Salerno, VP of Product, Brainshark

A roadmap conversation with a customer is an opportunity for a product person to verify their understanding of market needs before actually building the product. If you've done a really great job in your customer discovery, then the roadmap (in Steve Blank's words) is merely "confirming the mutual understanding" of these needs. It's also an opportunity to discover where you might be wrong, of course, which is perhaps even more valuable as you still have the opportunity to change direction (not so once the product is built).

But how do you protect against broken promises? Bob Levy, CEO of Virtual Cove, explains to customers up front that roadmap change is inevitable. "That's why we're having this conversation in the first place," he tells them. "We make our decisions based on input from people like yourself. You have the power to influence the roadmap, as do others, so of course it won't be the same when it's done. Customers are frustrated insomuch as they think a roadmap is a static thing."

Chapter 8 provides advice on sharing your roadmap with customers and other stakeholders and on how to present to these groups to get their buy-in.

► A Roadmap Should Not Make Promises a Team Cannot Deliver On

Problem: Your stakeholders and customer expect a firm commitment on dates for your product releases

In today's fast-paced and constantly changing world, there is a natural desire for certainty and predictability. In the past, roadmaps often read like a Gantt chart, with specific dates and commitments of features. However, because we now live in an agile—arguably post-agile—world, such commitments and dates are often missed, leaving customers and stakeholders disappointed.

Symptoms of this particular problem include:

- The roadmap includes a list of features and dates that are frequently unable to be realized.

- A product team is scrambling in the last few weeks/days toward product release.

Solution: Prioritization is critical to deliver on your commitments

A roadmap is a strategic document that should offer guidance to your teams on what to focus on. If your team has a track record of missing commitments, there's likely a prioritization and even an estimation problem—that is, the team cannot properly estimate what they can get done in a specific timeframe. Carol Meyers reiterates this point: "I think it's really hard for people to know how long it's actually going to take them, and I think it has led to a lot of discord among groups within companies about, 'You said you would deliver,' and then 'Well, we found out that technically this was a lot harder than we thought.'"

When teams are building something new, regardless of their skill set, it's a challenge to accurately predict the length of time it will take. But precise prioritization can help focus the team so they can make the most effective use of their time.

"We always seem to overpromise and underdeliver."

"It feels like we're constantly playing catch-up."

A Roadmap Should Not Require Wasteful Up-Front Design and Estimation

Problem: **Time spent estimating design and development efforts takes time away from actually implementing them**

Symptoms of this particular problem include:

- The roadmap includes a list of features that need to be "sized" or "estimated" for design and development.

- A product team is scrambling in the last few weeks/days toward product release.

Solution: **Let the teams determine the solutions, and allow them to solve the problem**

While we realize that some teams need to clearly define the product specification and deliver on it in a specific timeframe, the roadmap is intended as a strategy document. A project plan or a release plan may be better suited to outlining specific dates.

"My engineers hate giving estimates."

"We waste too much time arguing over how to solve something."

➤ A Roadmap Should Not Be Conflated with a Release Plan or a Project Plan

Problem: Your team looks at the roadmap as if it were a project plan listing when features will be released

A roadmap is a strategic artifact, whereas a release plan is a tactical artifact about execution.

Symptoms of this particular problem include:

- Your release plan looks like a Gantt chart with specific delivery dates.

- Your roadmap consists of a list of features and dates.

Solution: Commit to outcomes rather than output

If you're paying attention, you'll notice this is the same solution to a different problem mentioned earlier. We find that inexperienced product pros often jump to the solution. After all, we've been acculturated to have "the answer" since we were in kindergarten. It's a natural bias we all have—we want the answer and we want to be problem solvers. The issue is that we go right to the solution (output) rather than do what experienced product pros do, which is focus on the problem (outcome). To take it a step further, the smartest product pros ask what outcomes they're seeking and drive toward those.

"I try to keep my roadmap at a high level, but Sales always demands dates."

"I don't know how detailed my roadmap should be."

"How does my roadmap fit into our Agile methodology?"

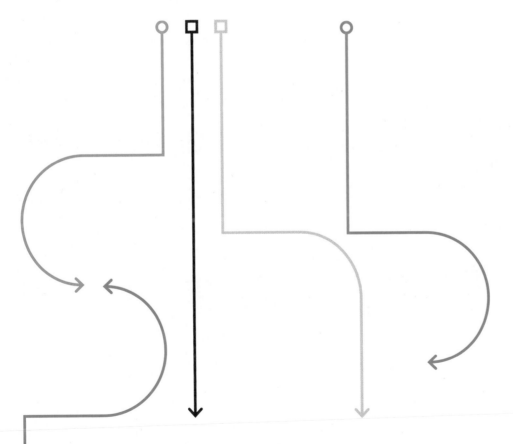

A roadmap is not a project plan.

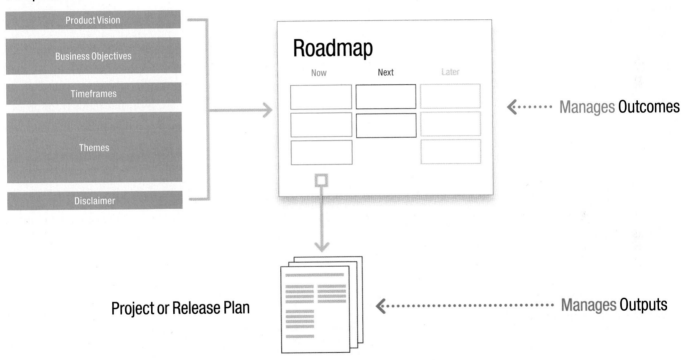

Components

Product Vision

Business Objectives

Timeframes

Themes

Disclaimer

Roadmap

Now   Next   Later

Manages Outcomes

Project or Release Plan

Manages Outputs

FIGURE 1-3. *A roadmap begins with a vision of where you're going and helps lead you there, with iterations and stops along the way*

Summary

Properly done, a product roadmap can steer your entire organization toward delivering on the company strategy. A good roadmap, though, is not so much a project plan as a strategic communications tool, a statement of intent and direction.

For many product people, product roadmaps have become a painful exercise in futility. The pace of change; lack of clear vision, goals, and internal alignment; and an excessive focus on feature and date specifics quickly obsolete their painstaking work, and this leaves them asking why they should invest the time in a roadmap at all.

In this chapter, we've laid out requirements for relaunching product roadmaps for a lean and agile world, including providing strategic context, focusing on value, embracing learning, rallying the organization, and getting customers to buy in. And all of this without making promises we can't keep, spending excessive time in up-front planning, or conflating the roadmap with more specifics-oriented documents like release and project plans.

Is this heroic feat possible? We've seen it in action at dozens of organizations around the world.

By first establishing guiding principles (including a product vision tied to your company vision and goals that will help measure your progress), by focusing on outcomes rather than features and dates, by prioritizing based on return on investment (ROI) in meeting your goals, by using input from all of your stakeholders to drive alignment, and by planning for and clearly communicating ongoing change, it's possible to set clear direction and simultaneously embrace the uncertainties inherent in product development today.

With that in mind, let's take a look at the components of a great roadmap and how they can help you make great products.

Chapter 2
Components of a Roadmap

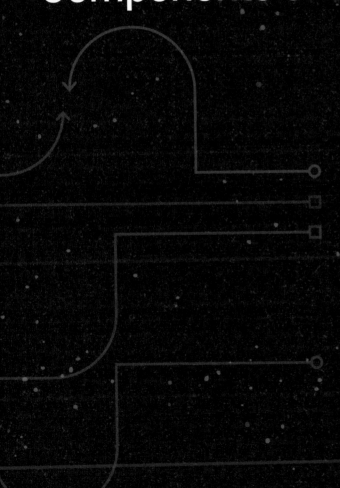

What you'll learn in this chapter

An Example Roadmap

The primary components for any product roadmap

- Product vision
- Business objectives
- Themes
- Timeframes
- Disclaimer

Secondary components to answer the concerns of certain stakeholders

- Features and solutions
- Confidence
- Stage of development
- Target customers
- Product areas

Complementary information to provide context for your roadmap

- Project information
- Platform considerations
- Financial context
- External drivers

Chapter

2

Components
of a Roadmap

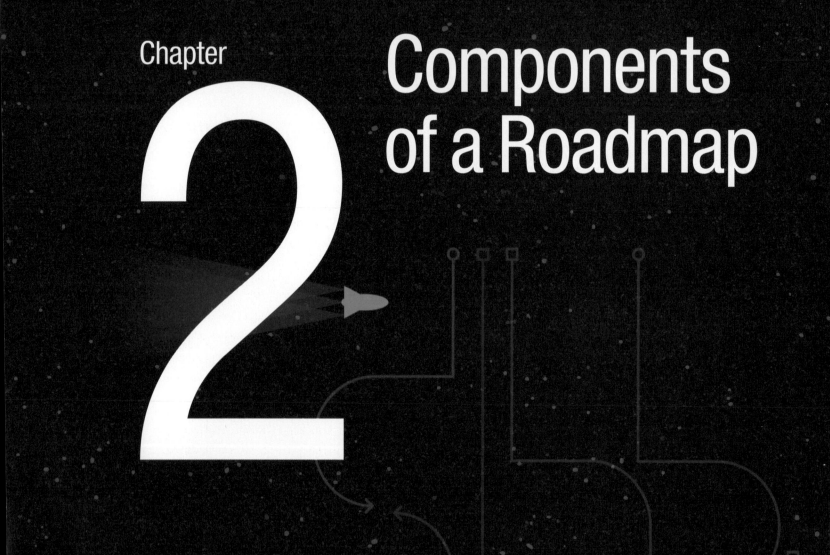

A document that can effectively rally your troops around a plan needs to be more than just a list of features and dates.

It needs to tell the story of what it will be like when you achieve your vision, what it will take to get there, and how you will know if you are making progress.

A lot of product people think of a roadmap as a simple chart with dates and features, but a document that can effectively rally your troops around a plan needs to be more than that. It needs to tell the story of what it will be like when you achieve your vision, what it will take to get there, and how you will know if you are making progress.

Every roadmap is different, and exactly what yours looks like will depend on what you are trying to communicate and to whom. There's no template or boilerplate you can plug-and-play for roadmap greatness, and a standardized roadmap doesn't work across all organizations.

In this chapter, we will explain each of these *primary roadmap components* using a simple (hypothetical) product roadmap for our favorite garden hose.

There are additional, *secondary components* we will explain and illustrate as well. These are optional, but will deepen your roadmap and help satisfy the specific concerns of some stakeholders such as your development team, sales and marketing teams, executives, etc.

Finally, there are groupings of related information we consider *complementary* to a roadmap. That is, they are not part of a roadmap formally, but may provide helpful context and help to tie the roadmap to the concerns of those same stakeholders.

We'll dig into each of these types of components in detail in subsequent chapters, but for now, let's have an overview and see how all the components come together to build a cohesive roadmap.

Primary Components

These components are necessary for an effective roadmap. Use this section as a checklist to ensure you've covered the essentials.

FIGURE 2-1. *Primary components of a roadmap*

Product Vision

Product Vision Is Your Guiding Principle

Whether they call it a mission, a vision, or a purpose, organizations usually have guiding principles that offer direction toward the proverbial North Star. We think of a *product* vision as how a specific sort of customer will benefit from your product when it is fully realized and ubiquitous.

Chapter 4 includes an in-depth explanation and real-world examples of guiding principles such as product vision.

Business Objectives

Business Objectives Help You Measure Progress

What are the goals your product will accomplish? The outcomes? What will be measurably different for your organization? These are powerful questions that will help you explain the why of your roadmap in concrete terms, get stakeholders excited about the future, and make it easier for you to get the resources you need.

As Bryan Dunn, VP Product Management at Localytics, says, it also gives them the freedom to ask, "What kind of product do we need in order to attain those business goals?"

Chapter 4 provides more depth on this topic, including an example of a roadmap driven primarily from business objectives.

 Timeframes

 Themes

 Disclaimer

Broad Timeframes Avoid Overcommitment

Focusing on dates as the primary measure of success diverts attention from the iterative and uncertain process of innovation so critical in new product development. Broad timeframes like calendar quarters or even Now, Next, and Later provide guidance while preserving some flexibility. In all cases, the sequence communicates what's important now and what can wait awhile.

Chapter 9 discusses when to include specific dates for external events and commitments, but we discourage you from including specific ship dates for the roadmap themes and solutions.

Themes Focus on Outcomes Rather Than Output

Answering the question "What would need to be true for our product to realize its vision and attain its business objectives?" is the best way we've found to organize the work and deliverables of your team. Expressing themes as customer needs or problems, in particular, is very effective in guiding the development of solutions (i.e., features and functions).

Chapter 5 discusses how to develop themes and subthemes, and provides real-world examples of theme-driven roadmaps.

The Disclaimer Protects You (and Your Customer)

Most roadmaps contain some sort of caveat just to make it absolutely clear that anything in the roadmap is subject to change without notice. This protects you from accusations of broken promises; it also protects your customer by making it clear that change is possible, even likely.

Disclaimers of large public companies are often more elaborate. Chip-making giant Intel publishes a roadmap that provides surprisingly little detail, but being a public company, they still preface it with a prominent disclaimer. Speak to your finance or legal department about your organization's policy here.

Meet the Wombat Garden Hose Co.

We'll use this hypothetical company to explain how components are used to create the simple roadmap shown here.*

*It's important to repeat that this is a very simple roadmap, used only to illustrate roadmap components. **This is not a roadmap template.** Roadmaps take many forms and will be highly customized to tell the story of what it will be like when you achieve your vision, what it will take to get there, and how you will know if you are making progress.*

As we said at the beginning of this chapter, there is no one roadmap format that will suit every product and every organization at every stage of growth. Still, we thought it would be useful to show you an example of how these elements could come together to tell a story of value for one product. And so the Wombat garden hose was born.

Imagine you work for a garden hose company and you've been asked to create a new product for affluent Americans. Where do you start?

Before we walk you through the thinking behind the creation of the Wombat roadmap, take a few minutes to review how the primary components are expressed in it.

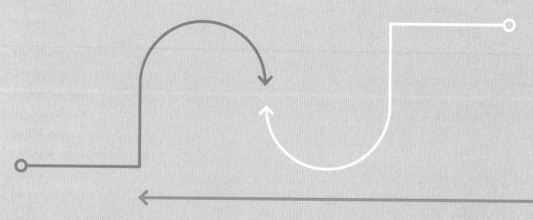

Product Vision

Our garden hose exists to help American consumers pursue the perfect landscapes they so seem to crave. The product vision directly reflects this in compact form, providing an effective framing for everything that comes after.

Timeframes

Our garden hose roadmap provides for wide half- and whole-year timeframes to ensure the team has the latitude to explore the best ways to solve customer problems.

Themes

The key problems customers face when watering their landscapes form the themes in the timetable at the heart of the roadmap

---

THE WOMBATTER Hose

PRODUCT VISION
Perfecting American lawns and landscapes by perfecting water delivery

H1'17	H2'17	2018	Future
Indestructible Hose Objectives: • Increase unit sales • Decrease number of returns • Decrease overall defects	**Delicate Flower Management** Objective: • Double ASP	**Putting Green Evenness for Lawns**	**Infinite Extensibility**
	Severe Weather Handling Objective: • NE Expansion	**Extended Reach**	**Fertilizer Delivery**

Updated 3/30/17, subject to change without notice.

Business Objectives

Each garden hose theme has one or a few objectives, each of them measuring the business improvement hoped for from solving the customer problems expressed in the theme.

Disclaimer

A simple date and "subject to change" notification at the bottom of the timetable is sufficient for the limited audience of this roadmap.

FIGURE 2-2. *The Wombat roadmap with primary components*

Developing the Wombat Roadmap

We start with the company vision, the reason we are developing products at all. This provides the grounding for everything that comes after (Figure 2-2).

Knowing that the company is focused on Americans and on making landscapes beautiful, you'd be in a good position to research what's most important to achieving this vision (Figure 2-3).

Armed with this insight (63% of Americans surveyed indicate insufficient irrigation…), your product vision would almost be written for you (Figure 2-4).

FIGURE 2-3. *The garden hose company's vision*

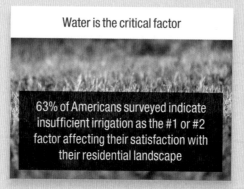

FIGURE 2-4. *What's most important to achieving the company vision*

FIGURE 2-5. *The product vision for the Wombat garden hose*

Work with potential customers should reveal the most important problems customers face in achieving their goal of perfectly-watered landscapes (Figure 2-5).

This set of problems could easily form a set of themes to guide your development efforts—and form the backbone of your roadmap (Figure 2-6).

Note how the first problem identified (hoses kink, split, and leak) maps directly to the first theme on the roadmap (indestructibility). Each subsequent theme then reflects the next prioritized problem.

The themes are ordered into broad timeframes, beginning with half-year periods and expanding to a single column for all of 2018. The final timeframe is simply "Future."

Additional details add color to each theme. Note that only one theme—the first—has any details about the features you'll actually ship. Carefully chosen diagrams, mockups, demos, or other exhibits of what you are planning to build make your ideas more tangible (Figure 2-8).

Water Delivery Problems

- Hoses kink, split, and leak
- Hoses harm delicate flowers
- Hoses self-destruct in severe weather
- Uneven distribution
- Limited range
- Fertilizer delivery is messy & complicated

FIGURE 2-6. *The most important problems customers face*

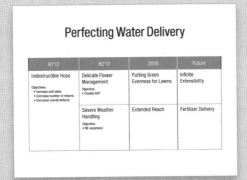

FIGURE 2-7. *The set of themes guiding the Wombat product roadmap*

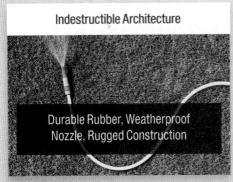

FIGURE 2-8 *Adding details and mockups to flesh out a theme*

Secondary Components

These components are optional but will enhance your roadmap in important ways for certain stakeholders. Every additional bit of information, however, has the potential to backfire.

Features and Solutions Show How You Intend to Deliver on Your Themes

Features and solutions are the specific deliverables that will fulfill the needs and solve the problems identified in the roadmap themes. These details are the new features, capabilities, quantities, enhancements, updates, or optimizations you will deliver. Depending on the expectations of your stakeholders, details may be very thin or include specifics such as product specs, architecture diagrams, flow diagrams, design sketches, or even prototypes.

See Chapter 6 for guidance on how to incorporate the proper details into your roadmap and tie them to themes effectively.

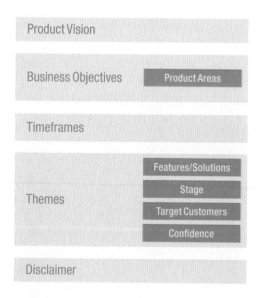

FIGURE 2-9. *Secondary components are typically related to a specific theme, but can appear anywhere on the roadmap.*

Stage of Development

Stakeholders seeing labels like "discovery," "design," or "prototyping" on a roadmap should understand that the product is in a very early stage of development. They may be able to see and provide input on sketches, layouts, material choices, and other design aspects before they are finalized. A label like "pre-production" or "beta," conversely, should convey that the product can be touched (or at least seen) and demonstrated, and is likely to be generally available soon.

See Chapter 6 for more examples of stage of development information in real-world roadmaps and for information on deepening your roadmap for an exploration and examples of each of these concepts.

See Chapter 9 on presenting and sharing your roadmap for more guidance on which stakeholders will benefit from which of these components.

Confidence

Indicating the level of confidence you have in your ability to address each item or theme on the roadmap in the next release is a great way to help offset the sentiment that once it's on paper (er… pixels?), it is a promise.

Target Customers

If your product serves more than one type of customer, it may make sense to call them out specifically on the roadmap.

Product Areas

A large and complex product—or a new product where basic functionality is still being laid down in many areas—may benefit from a roadmap where themes or features are annotated by product area. Individual product areas may also have separate business objectives.

Secondary Components Added to the Roadmap

Here we've added some of these secondary components to enrich and provide context for the Wombat roadmap. We haven't included all of them in this example. We think you will find that in practice, it's best to be selective, focusing on the key information needed by your stakeholders to provide context and no more. *See Chapter 6 for guidance on when to use each of these.*

1 **Features and Solutions**
Many product people are rightfully wary about sharing this level of detail with customers. Specific features are listed only for the indestructibility theme in the garden hose roadmap where the product is nearly ready for shipment. Later themes are too early in the development process to be that certain. For those, the problem expressed in the theme is the focus.

2 **Stage of Development**
Products in later stages of development are much more "real" to stakeholders like sales, marketing, customer support, and channel partners. The indestructible garden hose is in pre-production according to our fictitious roadmap, so these stakeholders should all be getting ready to market, sell, distribute, and support it.

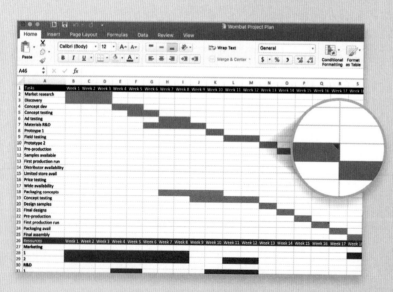

FIGURE 2-10. *The internal Wombat project plan contains far more detail on the precise timing and resources involved with the effort to deliver on the roadmap. Most roadmap stakeholders would find this level of information both overwhelming and distracting.*

3 Confidence

We chose not to place a confidence percentage on the Wombat roadmap. At Wombat HQ, we felt the stage of development information placed at the bottom of each theme through 2018 (and the lack of any such information in 2019), combined with the broad timeframes used here effectively communicated the tentative nature of the items further to the right. Percentages would add little more insight here.

4 Target Customers

It should be clear from the company vision and problem statement in the roadmap slides that the Wombat's initial offering will be focused on American consumers. However, the Infinite Extensibility and Fertilizer Delivery themes targeted for the future are aimed at the professional landscaper market and so this new target market is indicated.

THE WOMBATTER Hose

PRODUCT VISION
Perfecting American lawns and landscapes by perfecting water delivery

H1'17	H2'17	2018	Future
Indestructible Hose Objectives: • Increase unit sales • Decrease number of returns • Decrease overall defects Features: • 20' & 40' lengths • No-leak connections • No-kink armor **Stage:** Pre-production	**Delicate Flower Management** Objective: • Double ASP **Stage:** Prototype	**Putting Green Evenness for Lawns** **Stage:** Discovery	**Infinite Extensibility** Pro Market
	Severe Weather Handling Objective: • NE Expansion **Stage:** Materials Testing	**Extended Reach** **Stage:** Discovery	**Fertilizer Delivery** Pro Market

Updated 3/30/17, subject to change without notice.

5 Product Areas

Each theme for the Wombatter is being developed holistically by one team with no division between product components or areas. The roadmap therefore does not call out product areas, making for an uncluttered communication to stakeholders.

FIGURE 2-11. *The Wombat Roadmap with some secondary components added*

Complementary Information

These additional categories of information are not really part of a product roadmap; however, your stakeholders will expect you to be familiar with them and ready to discuss how things like hard external dates affect the roadmap. We include this list here so you can consider whether in some circumstances it may make sense to collaborate with your key stakeholders in a joint presentation that provides some of this information for context.

We'll discuss this concept in more depth in Chapter 9 on sharing and presenting your roadmap.

TABLE 2-1. *Complementary information can add color and context to a product roadmap*

	Category	Types of Information	Stakeholders
1	Project Information	Schedule, resources, status, dependencies, risks	Development team, executives
2	Platform Considerations	Scalability requirements, infrastructure needs, technical platform	Development team
3	Financial Information	Market opportunity, P&L	Executives, investors, board of directors
4	External Drivers	Regulatory changes, competition, events (e.g., conferences or trade shows)	Marketing, sales, channel partners, legal, compliance

Project Information

Because work on the Indestructible hose is actually in pre-production now, questions at the project execution level are natural.

A full production schedule is not part of the roadmap, but a quick mention of the number one risk can spark the right sort of conversation with internal stakeholders who may be able to help mitigate this risk.

Other complementary information can wait for other, target conversations on those topics with the right stakeholders.

THE WOMBATTER Hose

PRODUCT VISION
Perfecting American lawns and landscapes by perfecting water delivery

H1'17	H2'17	2018	Future

Indestructible Hose
 	
Objectives:
• Increase unit sales
• Decrease number of returns
• Decrease overall defects
 	
Features:
  • 20' & 40' lengths
  • No-leak connections
  • No-kink armor
 	
Stage: Pre-production
 	
In-Market Goal: May 31
 	
Risk:
Design overbooked in Feb
	Delicate Flower Management
	
	Objective:
	• Double ASP
	
	Stage: Prototype
		Putting Green Evenness for Lawns
		
		Stage: Discovery
			Infinite Extensibility
			
			Pro Market

	Severe Weather Handling Objective: • NE Expansion Stage: Materials Testing	**Extended Reach** Stage: Discovery	**Fertilizer Delivery** Pro Market

Updated 3/30/17, subject to change without notice.

FIGURE 2-12. *The Wombat Roadmap with some complementary information added*

Components in Context

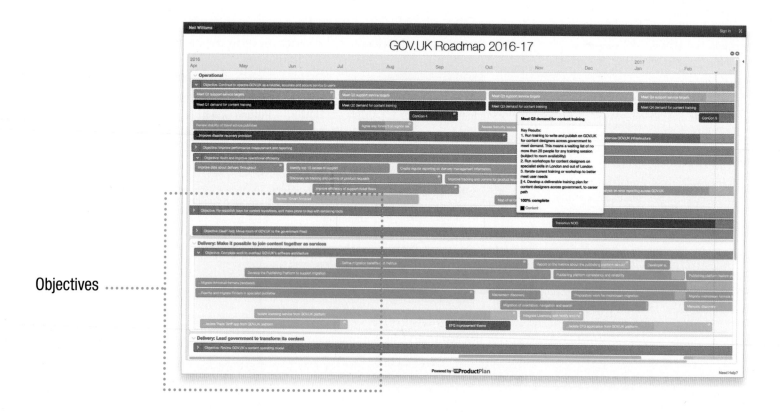

Objectives

FIGURE 2-13. *Gov.uk roadmap*

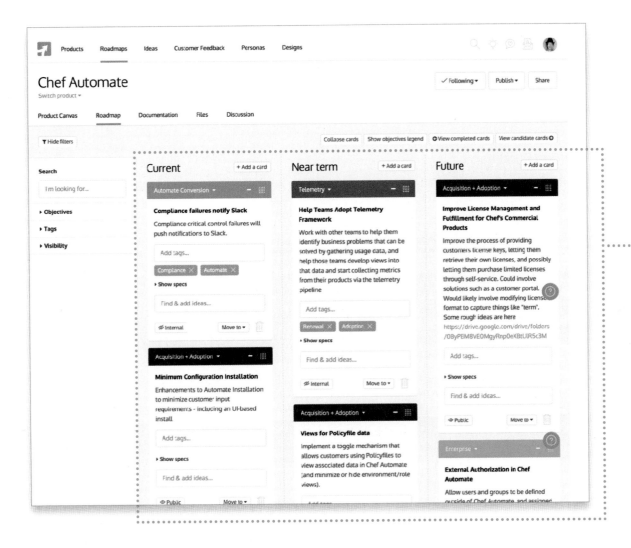

Themes

FIGURE 2-14. *Chef Automate roadmap*

Components in Context

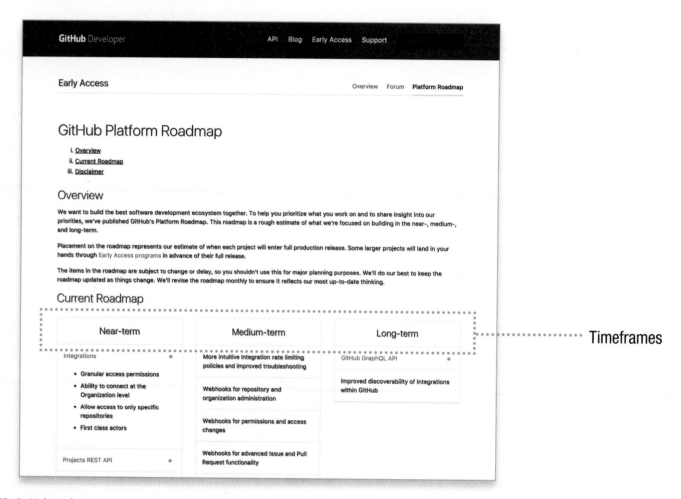

FIGURE 2-15. *GitHub roadmap*

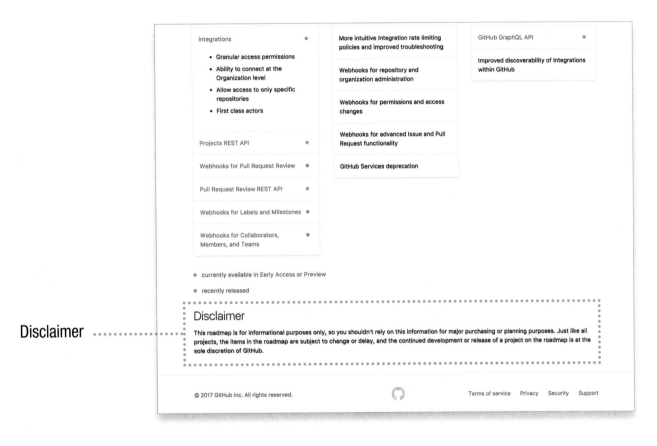

Disclaimer ································

FIGURE 2-16. *GitHub roadmap*

Components in Context

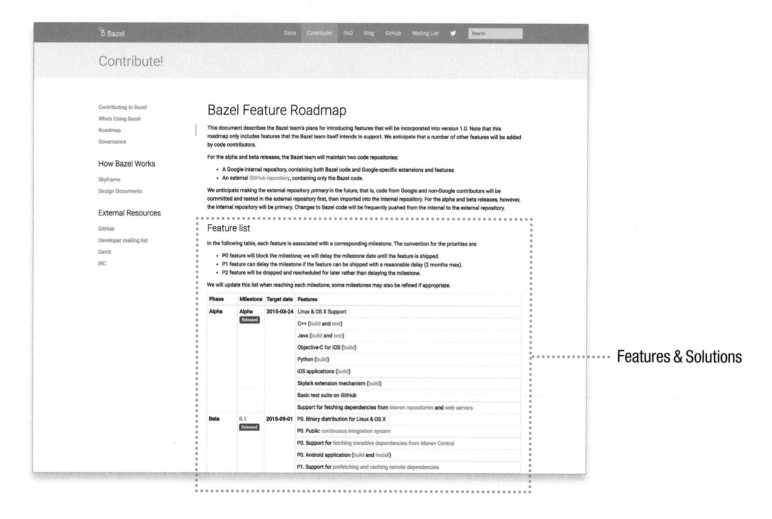

Features & Solutions

FIGURE 2-17. *Bazel roadmap*

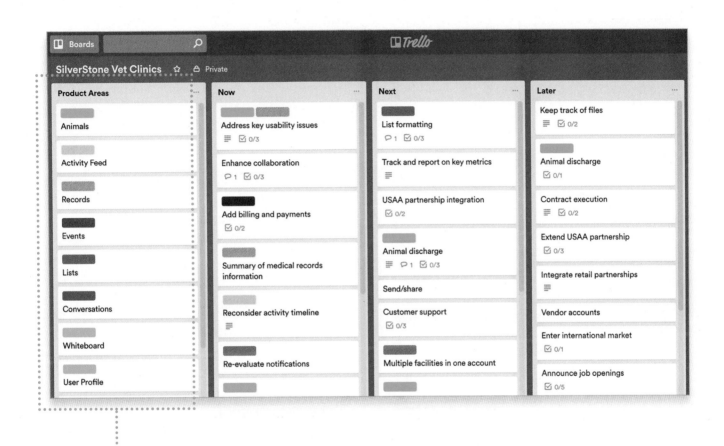

Product Areas

FIGURE 2-18. *Example roadmap*

Components in Context

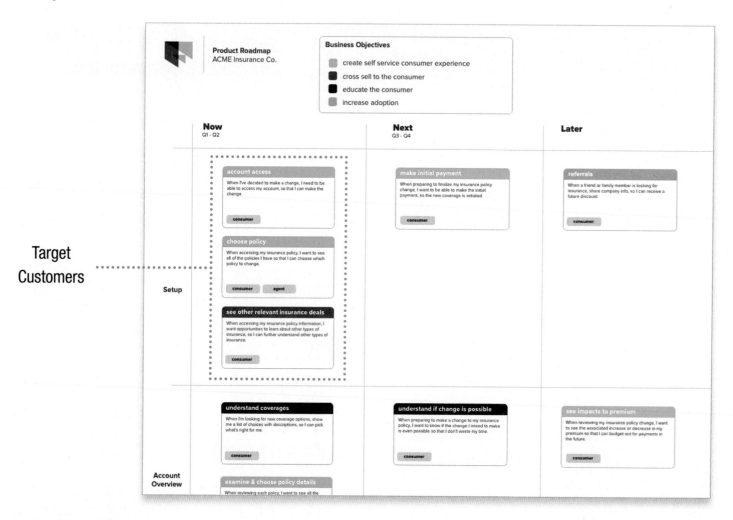

Target Customers

FIGURE 2-19. *Insurance company roadmap*

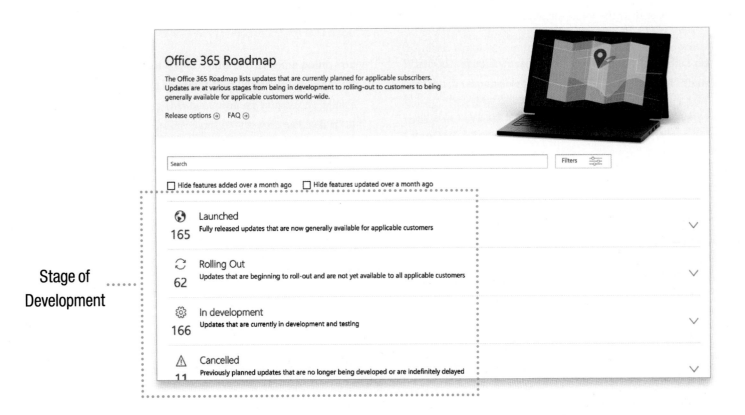

Stage of Development

Office 365 Roadmap

The Office 365 Roadmap lists updates that are currently planned for applicable subscribers. Updates are at various stages from being in development to rolling-out to customers to being generally available for applicable customers world-wide.

Release options ⊕   FAQ ⊕

Search   Filters

☐ Hide features added over a month ago   ☐ Hide features updated over a month ago

🌐 **Launched**
165   Fully released updates that are now generally available for applicable customers

🔄 **Rolling Out**
62   Updates that are beginning to roll-out and are not yet available to all applicable customers

⚙️ **In development**
166   Updates that are currently in development and testing

⚠️ **Cancelled**
11   Previously planned updates that are no longer being developed or are indefinitely delayed

FIGURE 2-20. *Office 365 roadmap*

Summary

Roadmaps come in many forms depending on the size and life cycle of the product. All, however, incorporate core concepts such as what is coming and approximately when (or at least in what order). The most effective ones provide context about why by including an explicit statement of product vision and a set of outcome-oriented themes, together with a disclaimer making it clear all of this is subject to change.

The best roadmaps don't obscure the core message with a lot of extraneous detail, but home in on the additional context most important to particular stakeholders.

See Chapter 9 on presenting and sharing for tips on choosing just the right details.

Now that you have a picture of what goes into a product roadmap, let's talk about where you can start.

Chapter 3

Gathering Inputs

What you'll learn in this chapter

What the different stages are in a product's life cycle

How to gather inputs from the market and business environment

How to gather input from your customers

How to gather input from your stakeholders

3

Gathering Inputs

Before you run off and make a roadmap, you'll need to spend some time gathering inputs.

The goal of gathering inputs is to make sure you have all of the relevant information and context you need to make good product decisions.

W ithout a constant refresh of that context, you'll risk making too many assumptions and mistakes. As part of this process you'll likely have lots of discussions and negotiations with your stakeholders.

Understand Where Your Product Is in Its Life Cycle

In the same way that a roadmap is relevant for all types of products, it's also useful at different stages in the life of a product. As we see it, there are five primary phases of a product's life cycle:

- New
- Growth
- Expansion
- Harvesting
- End of life

New Product Phase

In many cases we associate the new product state with startups, but there are a number of established companies putting time and resources into innovation and expansion in the new product realm. Your roadmap in this phase of the life cycle should be used to outline and drive the creation of the first version of your product.

With a new product, you are venturing into uncharted territory. This means you will have to make a lot of assumptions, and then rapidly prototype and test to get validation and answers. That validation, or lack thereof, will ultimately impact what themes or features make it onto your roadmap.

Growth Phase

The second phase in the life cycle is scaling an existing product. This means getting it to as many customers as possible. For example, when R. Colin Kennedy was Product Manager at Sonos, the objective for the year was to get as many product (speaker) installations as possible. The team was to focus on revenue, customer lifetime value, and so on, later—after scaling the product to get it into as many hands as possible.

Roadmapping here helps you prioritize the team's activities so all are operating to address scale. Sometimes this means a simple reorganization of features or themes to improve the user experience. In other cases you may actually remove features that are no longer necessary.

This phase is the most common for established businesses, as every company should be focused on—and its product roadmap geared to support—continual improvement.

As for risk and uncertainty, this stage tends to be low in both areas. Since the target customer base is known and you have a good understanding of their problems, product discovery is usually a bit smoother.

Product Expansion Phase

In the third phase we're focusing on here, a company uncovers an opportunity to expand the core product or product line into a new area. The new product opportunity is still linked to the core product, but it introduces fresh functionality and addresses an entirely new need. A good example is the popular flight aggregator site Kayak.com. When Kayak started, it did one simple thing: it allowed users to search for flights across multiple airlines at the same time, filter options, and compare costs. Once Kayak established itself in the market, it realized this format would also work for hotels and cars.

Harvesting Phase

The fourth life-cycle phase we want to mention is the "cash cow product" that simply needs to be maintained. In these cases, the product team has successfully found product-market fit, has usually been in the market for an extended period of time, and has a solid and growing base of customers. The product team has done a great job of delivering value, and for the most part users are happy. A good example here is Google AdWords. According to a 2016 article from *Investopedia*, "the bulk of Google's $75 billion revenue in 2015 came from its proprietary advertising service, Google AdWords," so it's clear AdWords is the definition of a cash cow product. We can suppose that the prime directive for the AdWords product team has been to keep the product useful and relevant, so customers keep coming back for more.

Product teams in this phase cannot sit back on their heels and simply rake in the profits. The more customers commit to a product, the more demanding they will become. Therefore, teams at this stage should have a constant and revolving roadmapping process that uses customer feedback to inform their decisions about what changes and continuous improvements to make.

End-of-Life Phase

The fifth and final life-cycle phase may feel a bit less relevant for the roadmapping process, but we assure you it requires a similar level of strategy and planning. This is the *sunsetting product* phase. Yes, it's disappointing to think about, but sometimes products fail (sad emoji). Most people think a roadmap is about progression and growth, and most often, that's the case. However, it can also be used to wind down and take a product off the market. Sunsetting a product can be a complicated and delicate task and usually requires a good deal of planning and alignment. Using a roadmap at the end-of-life phase is an incredibly useful way to wind down with ease, dignity, and strong communication across stakeholders.

Gathering Input from Your Market

Once you have a clear understanding of your product life cycle, it's time to look externally to learn about your market.

Understand Your Ecosystem

It seems obvious that to build a successful product, you need to comprehend the business ecosystem in which you operate, but in practice this understanding is frequently missing from product teams. Often we see that the product leader has sufficient knowledge of the business space, but the rest of the team does not. The designers, engineers, and other team members assume it's the product manager's responsibility to understand the business and to communicate strategy to the rest of the team. While this is true in theory, in practice we advise against it. In our opinion, every member of the team should have a basic understanding of the business environment.

If you don't do the work up front to truly study the business landscape, you start off with a faulty map. Like a 15th-century explorer trying to reach new lands with a map that shows only half the world, you can very easily end up in the wrong place.

There are a number of tools and techniques for gathering the business knowledge you need in order to think strategically about your product. We certainly can't review them all here, so we'll leave that to the more qualified consultants and world-class business schools. What we *can* do is recommend that, at a bare minimum, you assemble a basic business model analysis for your product. Business model templates like Alex Osterwalder's Business Model Canvas and Ash Maurya's Lean Canvas can guide you through this step. These tools help you identify and think strategically about the pillars of your business, such as:

- Problem and solution

- Value proposition

- Unfair advantage

- Key metrics

- Customer segments

- Distribution channels

- Costs

- Revenue model

- Key partners

- Key resources

We have found that the Lean Canvas is very effective for start-ups or new products, whereas the Business Model Canvas works well for existing products or growing businesses. That's just our opinion, though, and you should test a variety of tools to decide what works best for you and your team. If you can't complete one of these canvases at a basic level, you're certainly not ready to build your roadmap. Without this base level of understanding, you are starting your journey with partial information or too many assumptions, either of which is a recipe for disaster in product development.

Define the Problem and the Expected Outcome of the Solution

One very rough way to determine a product person's level of experience is that the novice focuses on features, while the seasoned pro focuses on problems. The best product pros take this to the next level and ask, "If we solve that problem, what's the outcome we want to see?" There's no better way to find that outcome than to understand your customer. Vanessa Ferranto, Director of Product at The Grommet, explains that this isn't as simple as you might expect: "You just want to get something out there in order to gather validated learning. Sometimes you're

successful, you see a positive outcome and you can continue to build on that. Sometimes the outcome is not what you expect and you have to revisit your approach."

In Steve Blank's Customer Development Model he stresses the importance of sequencing your exploration of the problem and solution, and the expected outcome.

He starts with Customer Discovery, which supports the criticality of understanding customer problems and needs. He expounds on the value of getting out of the building to validate the core problem you're addressing before you even think about moving to the next step. Often what a potential customer thinks is the problem is just a symptom of a much larger problem. Once the problem has been confirmed through direct interaction with your target audience, Steve's model moves onto Customer Validation, Customer Creation, and Company Building. The Customer Validation step requires you to prove that at least some of your target audience is willing to pay for your solution. The third step, Customer Creation, is about demonstrating your early success will lead to growing demand and a more sustained sales pipeline. Finally, according to Blank, Company Building happens when product and sales are strong enough to justify the expansion of the initial team into a more established company structure with formal departments.

Gathering Input from Your Customers

One of the most critical parts of effective product development is to properly identify who your customers are, and then to truly understand and empathize with them—their jobs, wants, needs, obstacles, frustrations, emotions, and more. If your product exists to solve a problem for someone, then you have to intimately know that "person" in order to address their needs. Doing so not only helps you validate *what* the problem is, but is also critical in understanding *how* best to solve it for them.

What this means is that every item on your product roadmap should address an actual customer need. And to address their needs, you need to understand their needs. Trying to roadmap without a deep level of empathy for your customer will invariably send you down the wrong path and waste your time. When this goes unchecked for too long, it eventually leads to product failure. Incorporating customer knowledge into your roadmapping process will ensure you're building the right things, for the right people, for the right reasons.

Customer Roles

Before we get into some suggestions about how to identify and empathize with your customer base, let's set some guidelines and clarify terminology.

From our perspective, ***user roles*** focus on jobs and functions. In other words, a user role describes the primary action taken by a particular user. For example, let's consider the popular online education platform Lynda.com. Lynda offers classes in business, software, technology, and creative skills to "help users achieve their personal and professional goals." Before building a platform, Lynda recognized a gap in the education market around professional skill development. Presumably, they realized many people wanted a way to enhance a skill set without having to attend in-person adult education classes. These traditional classes can be time-consuming and expensive, so the team at Lynda decided to provide a lightweight, remote option for functional education. If we take a very broad view of this problem area, we can immediately identify two roles: the student and the instructor. It's easy to see that in order for Lynda to successfully solve the problem, they needed to create a platform that would add value to both the student and the instructor roles.

User Types

The second term we want to clarify is **user type**. The user type addresses how a user will interact with your product, or defines a user's permissions in relation to the product. Common user types include:

- End user
- General admin
- Master admin
- Manager
- Operator
- Viewer

Users Versus Buyers

It's also important to differentiate between users and buyers. It may be obvious, but users *use* the product and buyers *buy* the product. In some cases, this is the same individual, but in other cases, it's not. In the enterprise or B2B world, it's often the case that the buyer is an entirely different person than the user. For example, the VP of Sales might decide to purchase an annual subscription to Salesforce.com, but it's most likely the sales

managers and sales reps who will use the product on a daily basis. In the consumer or B2C world, on the other hand, it's much more common for the buyer and user to be the same person. For example, a music lover may decide to purchase a monthly subscription to Spotify and will ultimately be the one that benefits from the service. In that case, one individual effectively represents both the buyer and the user.

To return to our Lynda.com example, we can assume that the student role's user type is "end user" because she will be using Lynda to take classes and learn new skills. We also recognize that she is a user *and* a buyer, because she'll not only be benefitting from the classes directly but also be paying for them out of her own pocket (see Table 3-1).

User role (who/do)		User type(s)
Student	To learn	End user, buyer

TABLE 3-1. *Lynda.com user role and type*

Roles Versus Personas

Finally, let's differentiate between user roles and user personas. Too often these two are conflated or misunderstood. It's important for the product pro to understand the difference and how they relate to each other.

A *persona* is often defined as a representation of a user that embodies the characteristics, feelings, and preferences of a user set. Personas deal with softer characteristics. They are typically depicted with a photo or image surrounded by descriptive characteristics and supporting attributes.

Personas are valuable because they help us to empathize with buyers and users. They allow us to put ourselves in an individual's shoes and see the problem from his or her point of view. The goal is not just to know who your customers are, but to truly understand them.

Roles help us categorize the different customers our product will help, and personas allow us to take our understanding to a deeper level. For example, if we consider again the role of the student, we can assume that every student who uses the Lynda platform will need to watch videos, download documents, ask questions in a forum, and so on. However, to create a really valuable experience for every kind of customer, we can use personas to uncover additional layers related to their needs. Professional Paul might need to download a history of payments so he can submit an expense report to his employer, who has agreed to cover the costs of his class. Or Social Sam might want to see detailed profiles of the other students in class so he can make friends through the network.

Let's connect all of this user talk back to the roadmap. Understanding your customer base in great detail helps you envision their needs and uncover the jobs that your product will need to help solve. In order to know what your users need, you first have to know who they are, what motivates them, and what actions they take. To do this, you must get out of the building and interact with them directly to understand what they're thinking, feeling, seeing, hearing, saying, and doing.

Gathering Input from Your Stakeholders

Up to this point, everything we've talked about in this chapter has been related to external factors—your users, their needs and behavior patterns, and the business environment in which your product will live. However, we also want to address an incredibly important internal factor as well. As a product person, you cannot build or grow your product in a vacuum, no matter how good your instincts are. You may be able to get a version 1 off the ground on your own, but going any further will require additional support. Therefore, your roadmapping process needs to incorporate collaboration from all key stakeholders.

First you need to identify all your stakeholders. At a bare minimum, most product teams are made up of a product manager, designers, and engineers. This small group is what we call the *product core* (see Figure 3-1). The product core is generally responsible for designing, building, shipping, and/or maintaining a particular product or version.

FIGURE 3-1. *A product core team consists of those who work directly on the product: Product Manager or Owner, designers, and engineers*

TABLE 3-2. *Stakeholders and how they benefit and contribute*

Stakeholder	Benefit	Contribute
Customers	Get excited about how they will benefit in the future	Provide feedback on value and priorities
Executives	Understand how resources are being used and potential ROI	Provide strategic context for product direction and priorities
Sales	Be ready to respond to questions about future product direction from customers and prospects	Provide feedback on what will make prospects buy and customers renew
Marketing & PR	Prepare for launch and promotion of future products or features	Provide feedback on what will get the attention of the target market
Customer Support	Be ready to respond to customer inquiries about bugs, usability issues, or future features	Provide feedback on the top reasons for support calls
Research	Plan research projects to support future roadmap themes	Provide information about the market and users to inform themes and priorities
Other Product Teams	Sync their technical approach and release schedule with your team	Sync your technical approach and release schedule with their team
Operations, Production, Purchasing, HR	Understand future infrastructure, tooling, plant, personnel, and other scaling needs	Provide insight into infrastructure, tooling, plant, personnel, and other costs of proposed roadmap items
Finance	Understand planned spending and expected ROI	Provide feedback on available budget and ROI targets
Vendors & Technology Partners	Plan for timing and volume of required components & supplies, performance specs	Provide feedback on capacity and performance specs, provide insight into new materials and technologies
Channel Partners	Plan assortment, pricing, promotion, training & distribution	Provide feedback on what will likely sell, timing & pricing; plan co-marketing

However, throughout the life cycle and development of a product, the core needs to work in conjunction with many other stakeholders, who contribute to the roadmap (see Table 3-2, previous page).

For small or early-stage organizations, the group of stakeholders should be small. However, as the product and its influence grow, additional layers of collaboration and support will be needed. You might envision these as rings surrounding your product. How these layers or rings are defined, and which stakeholders populate them, will depend entirely on the structure of your team and business.

For example, the rings might represent knowledge of the product space or customer base, influence over decisions, or even frequency of interaction with the product team—which is the example we're using here to demonstrate a typical hierarchy of the groups and individuals associated with the creation, adoption, and management of the product roadmap (see Figure 3-2). Ultimately, you will need to define how your collection of stakeholders should be organized, and how you will interact with them.

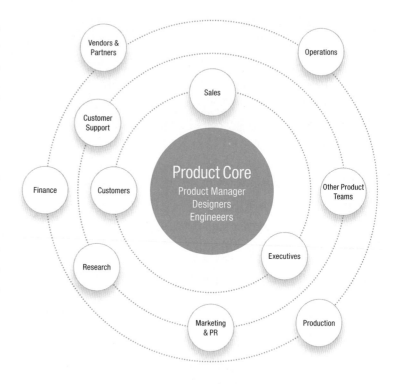

FIGURE 3-2. *The product core typically designs, builds, ships, and/or maintains a particular product or version*

"Each customer-facing team creates their own top-10 list and then all those teams merge their lists together to come up with an overall prioritized list representing the Voice of the Customer," says Jackie Bavaro, Head of Product Management at Asana. "Those lists are helpful when understanding what our internal stakeholders would like to see. This process ensures that each team gets to share their unique perspective, and the merging process empowers the teams to be directly involved in the ranking. Once I have that list, I then uplevel from specific feature suggestions into broader themes and consider additional tactical and strategic factors to determine the roadmap."

We'll talk more about stakeholders in Chapter 8, but in the beginning it's very important to identify who your stakeholders are. As you do, make sure to identify the role they will play in the development of the product.

At different points throughout the roadmapping process, you'll bring these individuals into the conversation. Your commitment to involving stakeholders will greatly improve the quality of your product, and also make the road to building it much smoother.

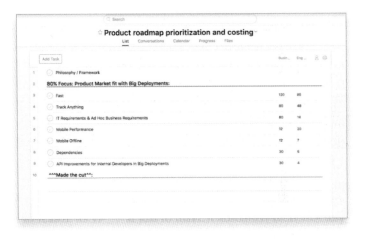

FIGURE 3-3. *Product roadmap prioritization and costing example*

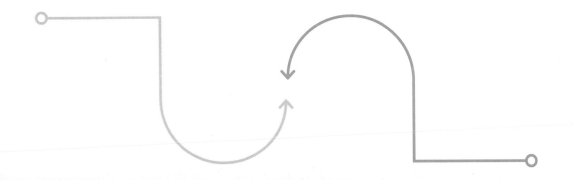

Summary

Trying to create a product roadmap without a basic understanding of the product's domain and its users will leave you groping around in the dark designing for fictional scenarios with biased assumptions. As you can imagine, this is a risky path to tread. Falling prey to the hubris convincing you that you already have all the context you need will result in wasted time, effort, resources, and of course money. So, to put it plainly: do the up-front work to gather or update the key inputs we've mentioned so you can be informed and prepared to build winning products.

The aforementioned inputs are not intended to encompass every bit of context you need prior to embarking on your roadmap effort, but they are the most important ones. There are other things, like full comprehension of the current or intended technology stack, that you'll want to have a grasp of as well. A good way to think about this is, the more information you have about the space in which you are operating, the more effective you will be as a product leader. Your role will require you to make sense of all of these inputs, interpret how they will affect the product, and then build that knowledge into your roadmapping process.

Chapter 4

Establishing the Why with Product Vision and Strategy

What you'll learn in this chapter

The difference between mission, vision, and values

How to create and communicate your product vision

How to develop a product strategy for achieving your vision

The importance of defining metrics for success

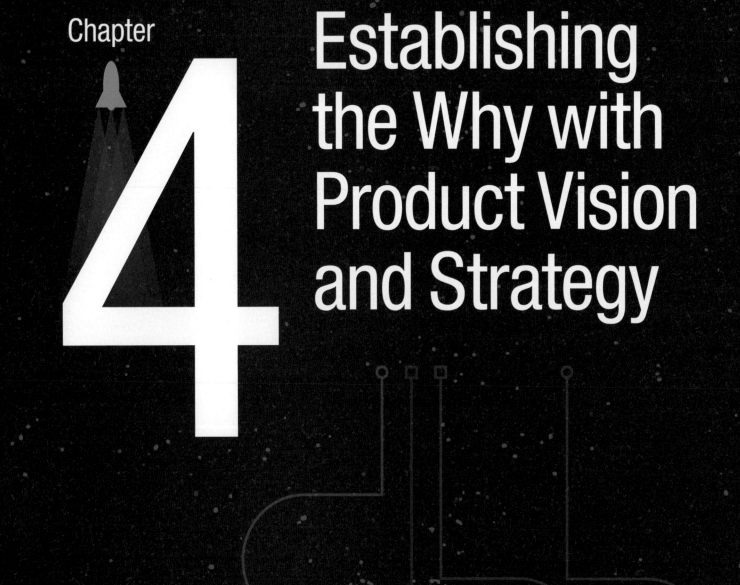

Chapter

4

Establishing the Why with Product Vision and Strategy

A product vision should be about having an impact on the lives of the people your product serves, as well as on your organization.

It's easy to get overwhelmed by the various concepts and terminology surrounding product development, and even more when you start to consider the terminology involved with strategy.

There are mission statements, company visions, values, goals, strategy, problem statements, purpose statements, and success criteria. Further, there are acronyms like KPI and OKR, which also seem potentially useful in guiding your efforts. How do you know which ideas apply to your situation, and where to start?

Whether your organization is mission-, vision-, or values-driven (or a combination thereof), these are all considered guiding principles to draw from and offer your team direction. For the purposes of this book, we'll establish definitions for *mission*, *vision*, and *values*, so we have a common language. Bear with us if you have different definitions of them yourself.

Mission Defines Your Intent

A *mission* is not what you value, nor is it a vision for the future; it's the intent you hold right now and the purpose driving you to realize your vision. A well-written mission statement will clarify your business's intentions. Most often we find mission statements contain a mix of realism and optimism, which are sometimes at odds with each other.

There are four key elements to a well-crafted mission statement:

Value

What value does your mission bring to the world?

Inspiration

How does your mission inspire your team to make the vision a reality?

Plausibility

Is your mission realistic and achievable? If not, it's disheartening, and people won't be willing to work at it. If it seems achievable, however, people will work their tails off to make it happen.

Specificity

Is your mission specific to your business, industry, and/or sector? Make sure it's relevant and resonates with the organization.

Here are two example missions. Can you guess the company for either?

Company A

To refresh the world…
To inspire moments of optimism and happiness…
To create value and make a difference.

Company B

To inspire and nurture the human spirit—one person, one cup, and one neighborhood at a time.

Company A is Coca-Cola, and Company B is Starbucks. While these missions may also be considered marketing slogans due to the size and popularity of each company, it's important to note their aspirational context.

Another aspect of mission that's often overlooked is that it has to reflect what you do *for someone else.* That someone else is typically not your shareholders, but your customers.

Vision statements are very often conflated with mission. We've seen many company vision statements that are actually mission statements. Vision statements are a challenge to not be self-centered to "be the best ___."

Vision Is the Outcome You Seek

A company *vision* should be about a longer-term outcome that has an impact on the lives of the people your product serves, as well as on your organization. Vision is why your organization exists, and it can be decomposed into the benefits you hope to create through your efforts—for both the world and your organization. It can be a literal vision of the future, such as "create a world where you can belong anywhere" (Airbnb) or "become a multi-planet species" (SpaceX), or "A just world without poverty" (Oxfam).

In its simplest form, a company vision is a statement that paints a future reality or world. A solid vision statement will address, at minimum, these two aspects:

- The target customer—the *who?*
- The benefit or need(s) addressed—the *why?*

Some might include a third:

- What makes it unique—*how is it different?*

Let's take the earlier example from Airbnb:

Create a world where you can belong anywhere.
- *Who?* You, the customer!
- *What?* A sense of belonging.
- *How it's different?* Anywhere in the world, even if you don't feel like you belong there.

Values Are Beliefs and Ideals

Values are also intended to guide behaviors. Values shape that ambiguous word thrown around company HR departments, *culture*—how people behave when no one is watching. Your organization's values may inform your vision or mission, and how you go about achieving it.

Values are often referred to as your *compass*. A compass tells you which direction is north or south, but not which direction to travel; you must make that decision yourself. Likewise, your values will help you determine what's right or wrong for your business, but not which direction to take—that's where your vision and mission come in.

Your vision is your ultimate destination, and your mission tells you which direction to follow in order to reach that destination. Take InVision App's values as an example: "Question Assumptions. Think Deeply. Iterate as a Lifestyle. Details, Details. Design is Everywhere. Integrity." They give employees a guide for how to make decisions during their work.

Here's a simple example: if you were a buyer at Whole Foods Market, a large organic grocery store primarily in the United States (and recently acquired by Amazon), and you followed the value "We Sell the Highest Quality Natural and Organic Products Available," would you select foods that contain artificial ingredients to stock in the stores? We would hope not, as that value ought to tell you that's the wrong direction for the company.

Most roadmaps provide a lot of detail about what you intend to deliver without the context of a vision, mission, or values. When you first establish that foundation by outlining your vision and your strategy for pursuing it, the details you provide—within the themes, features, functions, deliverables, services, activities, and so on—will paint a clearer picture to all the stakeholders of your roadmap. They will support and contribute to that foundation, rather than carrying the burden themselves in hopes that stakeholders will piece everything together on their own.

With these concepts defined, now let's talk more in depth about how they inform your product roadmap.

Product Vision: Why Your Product Exists

Product vision clarifies why you are bringing a product to market in the first place, and what its success will mean to the world and to the organization. The vision is the *raison d'être* of the entire effort, and forms the basis of the roadmap. As we mentioned previously for vision, it is the destination you plan to reach.

Capella University was an early innovator in online higher education. Its initial success came from delivering high-quality online learning experiences, but as others began to follow suit, they needed to differentiate their offerings.

A key insight came when they discovered that even one personal connection dramatically reduced the student's likelihood of dropping out, and that online access to financial aid and similar resources reduced volumes of phone calls to support hotlines and resulted in more satisfied students. This led them to a product vision of "delivering the entire university experience successfully over the web," according to Jason Scherschligt, who managed Capella's online experience. Critically, this vision included not just access to academic learning spaces, but also administrative functionality, support resources (tech support, a career center, writing resources, disability services, and an online library), and a private network of fellow learners, faculty, and alumni.

"The vision work was critical to the success of this initiative," explains Scherschligt. "While it started as just an upgrade of an ERP [Enterprise Resource Planning] portal, it became a much more valuable property for the organization through strong vision and storytelling. We initially conceived of the initiative in 2008, launched the first release in June of 2009, and it remains at the heart of the Capella online experience."

A clear product vision made it straightforward for Scherschligt and his team to tie every decision and every priority to the result they wanted for students—a full university experience via the web—and to develop what we call "themes" based on those desired outcomes.

It's likely that someone, somewhere in your organization, has a product vision. This does nobody any good if it remains stuck in that person's head. If your CEO has a vision but she doesn't communicate it to the rest of the organization, you can bet there will be struggles when it comes time to make decisions and she's not present.

If your organization has multiple products, the product vision is likely different from the corporate vision, though still supportive of and derived from it. For example, Google Search's product vision is "to provide access to the world's information in one click." It's easy to see how that comes directly from the broader company mission: "to organize the world's information and make it universally accessible and useful."

To create a product vision we suggest starting with Geoffrey Moore's "Value Proposition template" (also known as the "Elevator Pitch template") from his book, Crossing the Chasm (HarperBusiness). We have adapted it slightly for use in product roadmapping.

Value Proposition Template

For: [*target customer*]

Who: [*target customer's needs*]

The: [*product name*]

Is a: [*product category*]

That: [*product benefit/reason to buy*]

Unlike: [*competitors*]

Our product: [*differentiation*]

Example for Our Wombat Hose

For homeowner landscape enthusiasts

Who need a reliable hose that's survives repeated use

The Wombat Garden Hose

Is a water delivery system

That offers a reliable operation under any conditions

Unlike the competition

The Wombat Garden Hose is indestructible and offers uninterrupted water delivery

Then take this one step further and tie this sentence to your company's strategy by adding a description:

Supports our: [*objective(s)*]

Finally, to pare this down to a vision statement, try to compress that information into the following:

A world where the [*target customer*] no longer suffers from the [*identified problem*] because of [*product*] they [*benefit*].

Wombat Garden Hose Example:

> A world where American landscape enthusiasts [*target customer*] can have a more predictable and automatic [*identified problem*] watering system that can perfect their lawns [*benefit*] with an effective water delivery system [*product*].

This focuses on the *who* (target customer), the *what* (problem it solves), and the *why* (benefit they receive). Additionally, it also helps to write out all the preceding information in order to arrive at a clear product vision. We realize this can seem formulaic, and there is a downside to a vision statement that's plug-and-play when it should be unique and specific to your product and business. However, this template is a great tool when you are starting from scratch, or if you have established a product vision and need a gut-check to determine if you have something robust to drive your product strategy and roadmap.

Some product teams will pare this even further to just the product benefit and product differentiator.

To [*benefit realized*] by [*product differentiator*]

Wombat Garden Hose Example:

> To perfect American lawns by perfecting water delivery.

"When done well, the product vision is one of our most effective recruiting tools, and it serves to motivate the people on your teams to come to work every day. Strong technology people are drawn to an inspiring vision; they want to work on something meaningful."

—Marty Cagan, founder of Silicon Valley Product Group and author of Inspired

Duality of Company and Customer Benefit

While we're discussing vision, let's not forget the organization's perspective. A vision of company success might be to "operate the best omni-channel specialty retail business in America" (Barnes & Noble) or to be "a major platform player like Salesforce and Hubspot" (Contactually). An internal vision like this is just as important as an externally motivated one. They work together symbiotically to make something great.

Acknowledging that you need to make money to stay in business and deliver on your vision of a better world is healthy, and it allows you to have open discussions of ideas that serve both or only one of those visions.

One caution about internal vision statements, however, is that they can become too company-focused and fail to include the customer. Microsoft's famous vision of "a personal computer on every desk running Microsoft software" from the 1980s is a great example. At that time, it described a future aspirational world where the benefit to Microsoft is apparent, but inherent to that is a benefit to each individual by having a computer at their desk. One could argue that this vision fails is in service to Microsoft's customers and is too centric to Microsoft. As we're writing this book using a combination of MacBooks, tablets, and desktop computers, we're fully aware of the benefit of a personal computer. Today that benefit is clear, but in 1980s it came with an implied customer benefit, so it worked. Today that vision could fall short since it's too Microsoft-centric and times have changed with respect to a computer on everyone's desk (it's now in your pocket, and soon to be ubiquitous). As you can imagine, it no longer is Microsoft's vision as of the writing of this book.

Product Strategy:
How You Achieve Your Vision

Your product strategy is the bridge that connects your high-level vision to the specifics of your roadmap. And for many companies, the product strategy is the main contributor to their overall business strategy. This makes it crucial that you use product strategy as a starting place for your roadmap.

If your product vision includes meeting the needs of a group of people, then your product strategy simply makes that more explicit and concrete by explaining a bit about how. Usually, this takes the form of objectives. For example, SpaceX hopes to meet its lofty (literally) vision of "make going to Mars a reality in your lifetime."

To ensure that its relationship marketing platform is financially viable, Contactually has defined business objectives for increasing the number of sales leads, average sale price, trial conversion, and customer retention.

Furthermore, Contactually has effectively combined internal and external business objectives in its themes. Its *business* strategy is to grow in "the real estate professional market for the coming year," while planning "to expand into other segments in the future." This business strategy allows Contactually to combine the market's needs with its own. Let's convert this to *product* strategy, and see how it's separate, but very related to, business objectives.

Objectives and Key Results

Identifying business objectives that tie to your vision is critical to making that vision a reality. It's great to say, "We imagine a world where instant teleportation from one location to another makes travel options effortless." However, if you don't have specific objectives to hit along the way, that vision will be challenging to implement because there will be too many different product, technology, and business directions to take to get there. (Though if you do make teleportation a reality, please tell us; we collectively have too many frequent flyer miles!)

Often referred to as **objectives and key results (OKRs)** are a great way to pair your business objectives with success criteria. The premise of the OKR framework is that *objectives* are specific qualitative goals, and *key results* are quantitative measures of progress toward achieving those objectives. The first implementation of OKRs was by Andrew Grove at Intel in the early 1980s, as he recounts in his book *High Output Management* (Vintage). Many well-known organizations—Google, Uber, Zynga, and LinkedIn, to just name a few—utilize OKRs in their operations today. Christina Wodtke, author of *Radical Focus* (Boxes & Arrows), adopted the OKR framework to set personal goals and also wrote a short ebook dedicated to OKRs for products.

Here are a few guidelines on OKRs as they apply to product roadmapping:

- Everything on the roadmap must be tied to at least one of your objectives.

- Stick to a manageable number of objectives; from our experience and research, fewer than five seems to be most effective.

- Focus on outcomes, not output.

We've interviewed dozes of teams and have found that while every product team has unique metrics, there are some patterns.

The 10 universal business objectives

We've distilled every business objective we've encountered into a list of 10 that can apply to just about any product, regardless of whether it is a hardware, software, or service product. Whenever we ask "why" enough times about a proposed roadmap theme, feature, solution, program, or other initiative, it always seems to come back to one of these underlying objectives.

For each of these universal objectives, we've listed a Wombat Garden Hose theme, solution, or other initiative that might have been motivated by that underlying objective. We've also suggested a key result that could be used to measure success in reaching that objective.

Your product is likely to have an organizational objective (or two, or five) that resembles any of these. Note that these are not customer-facing goals, yet internal and customer-focused objectives should be mutually reinforcing (we'll talk more about customer-facing goals in Chapter 5). Bryan Dunn, VP Product Management at Localytics, poses a great question, "What kind of product do we need to attain those business objectives?" For example, work on improved usability will increase customer lifetime value (LTV) by decreasing churn. The goal for the customer is a better user experience; the goal for the product is decreased churn and increased LTV. The duality we mentioned previously is balanced.

Universal Objective	Wombat Theme or Solution	Wombat Key Result
Sustainable Value		
Support the product's core value	Indestructibility	Must-have for first ship
Create barriers to competition	Branded proprietary materials	Must-have for first ship
Growth		
Grow market share	Competitive trade-in program	5% share in first season
Fulfill more demand	Bring another plant online	Reduce out-of-stock incidents to <10%
Develop new markets	Contractor version	200k contractor unit sales in first season
Improve recurring revenue	Consumable add-ons	65% repurchase rate
Profit		
Support higher prices	10-year warranty	20% price increase does not reduce unit volume >5%
Improve lifetime value	Proprietary connectors discourage mixing brands	Average LTV +30% in second season
Lower costs	Bring packaging in house	Reduce finished product cost by 15% in 12 months
Leverage existing assets	Develop white-label version for other brands	Generate >$1m with unused plant capacity in first 12 months

TABLE 4-1. *The 10 universal business objectives*

Let's take this back to the Contactually example. It expresses its *product* strategy for the next year in three objectives, each with measurable success criteria:

1. "launch new features or services that realtors will pay more money for,"
2. "improve the feature sets of our existing plans so more users will purchase,"
3. "improve our team functionality to better meet the needs of team leads."

Each of these themes is tied to an objective that can then be measured by specific key results, and their roadmap reflects this. This internal objectives-driven approach to roadmapping makes direction crystal-clear for internal teams. In this case, rather than being based on customer needs, each objective focuses on a measurable business benefit that work is designed to achieve (higher average sale price or higher renewal rate, for example). This "outcome-based" roadmap makes clear why certain work is important, even allowing Contactually to leave placeholders for features yet to be conceived. This framework also makes room for things not often included on product roadmaps, such as bug fixes and infrastructure enhancements, by providing the business justification for that work.

See Chapters 5 and 6 for more information on identifying and solving for customer needs.

This Contactually roadmap is designed to support internal discussions about business objectives and how much of the company's resources are allocated to each. The specific deliverables in each month are comparatively downplayed as those are the outputs (more on this in a minute).

A roadmap based primarily on internal business objectives would not, of course, be appropriate for sharing with customers or channel partners. Customers are not interested in your internal metrics or your effort to develop a new technical platform; they care only about how you will add value to them or their business. These external stakeholders are equally uninterested in your resource allocation—unless it shows them that you are focusing a substantial set of resources on their favorite problem or feature idea.

All this begs the question: how you do know if you have achieved those objectives? You have metrics to track your progress. And who doesn't love a good metric?

When this roadmap was composed, the September customer development work was already complete, allowing good definition of the work planned for the next two months.

Definition of the next major effort, however, is explicitly postponed until customer feedback from the previous work can be assessed and new needs identified.

The second column describes the business outcome the company is looking for and what general class of work is planned to achieve that outcome. We would call these "objectives."

The first column indicates the percentage of resources allocated to each outcome.

Investment in infrastructure is explicitly called out. Note the outcome is described as a business benefit: "to iterate and differentiate faster."

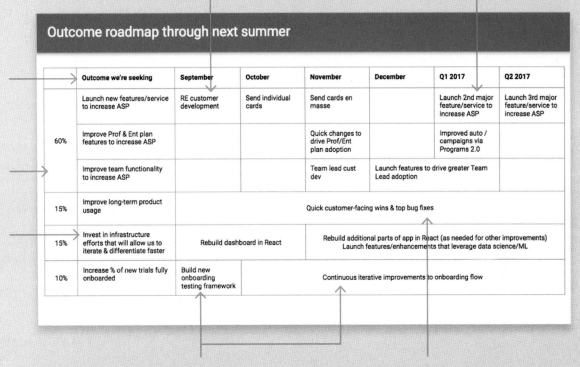

Outcome roadmap through next summer

	Outcome we're seeking	September	October	November	December	Q1 2017	Q2 2017
	Launch new features/service to increase ASP	RE customer development	Send individual cards	Send cards en masse		Launch 2nd major feature/service to increase ASP	Launch 3rd major feature/service to increase ASP
60%	Improve Prof & Ent plan features to increase ASP			Quick changes to drive Prof/Ent plan adoption		Improved auto / campaigns via Programs 2.0	
	Improve team functionality to increase ASP			Team lead cust dev	Launch features to drive greater Team Lead adoption		
15%	Improve long-term product usage	Quick customer-facing wins & top bug fixes					
15%	Invest in infrastructure efforts that will allow us to iterate & differentiate faster	Rebuild dashboard in React		Rebuild additional parts of app in React (as needed for other improvements) Launch features/enhancements that leverage data science/ML			
10%	Increase % of new trials fully onboarded	Build new onboarding testing framework	Continuous iterative improvements to onboarding flow				

Some near-term work is described very specifically because it is well-understood. Later work is described in more general terms, reflecting the reality that needs will emerge over time.

Many companies divert resources for critical customer complaints or demands out of necessity. Planning for it on your roadmap makes room for that work without disrupting your other plans and commitments.

FIGURE 4-1. *Contactually's outcome-based roadmap*

Key results (and metrics)

One of the most important things a product pro must do before releasing a product is define how the success of that product will be measured, or its *key performance indicators* (KPIs). These KPIs are often the metrics you are using to measure the *key results* from your OKRs. They are data that give you meaningful feedback on how your product is doing. The process of choosing which metrics to capture can be complicated, and you'll benefit greatly from exposure and experience. For the new product person, we have one key piece of advice here: find a balance with the amount of data you analyze. Three to five objectives are usually sufficient, and the metrics to measure them shouldn't be exponential. Sometimes you might have only one metric. (Your mileage may vary, but remember that the more objectives, the less focus you can likely give them. See Chapter 7 if you need help prioritizing.) If it takes you longer than one hour to review your data at a high level each week, we would argue you're trying to track and interpret too many metrics. Data analysis is an important part of your product roadmapping process, but you don't want it to be so onerous that it consumes too much time.

As your product grows and as your product team gets better and better at testing solutions and improving functionality, your approach to data collection can always become more sophisticated. All that said, you also have to make sure to define enough success metrics to actually be able to capture valuable insights. Just tracking revenue is not going to cut it if you want to create a product that provides lasting value. A metric like revenue alone will certainly tell you something's not working, but only when it's too late. In our experience, starting with a handful of KPIs is a good and manageable place to land.

In addition to specific product metrics, incorporating customer feedback can give you a more robust picture of your users' behaviors. You've probably heard of the *net promoter score* as a quantitative measure of qualitative customer feedback. There's no substitute for talking to your customers face-to-face and listening to them talk about how they use, like, and/or dislike your product. This combination of quantitative and qualitative data is powerful when executed well. Once you have a reliable system for defining what to track and analyzing your results, you can use that information to inform and prioritize your roadmap.

Tying this back to Contactually's objective of "improve the feature sets of our existing plans so more users will purchase," key results here could be "an increase in user base by 5% over the course of a specific timeframe" (a quarter, year, etc.) and feature-specific metrics such as "time to compose and send an email is reduced by 10%," indicating that the usability of that part of the product has been improved. Note that there can be multiple key results to each objective, as it may take different measures to determine whether an objective is met.

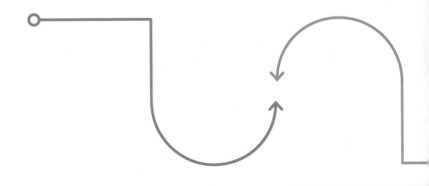

Outcome Versus Output

Well-known *Harvard Business Review* blogger Deb Mills-Scofield gives a great example distinguishing what you're delivering (output) from the reasons why (outcome): "Let's define outputs as the stuff we produce, be it physical or virtual, for a specific type of customer—say, car seats for babies. And let's define outcomes as the difference our stuff makes—keeping your child safe in the car." Her summary is the best way to keep these terms straight: "Outcomes are the difference made by the outputs."

We've said several times that your roadmap should focus on outcomes over outputs. Nonetheless, sometimes you will be required to provide more concrete detail about what you plan to deliver as part of your strategy for achieving your vision. SpaceX showed diagrams of spacecraft designs and videos of Mars landings to provide a taste of what it intends to deliver. Video game companies like Nintendo are famous for cinematic trailers designed to whet players' appetites without committing to details. Electronic component manufacturers frequently provide specs months or even years in advance to their OEM partners, on the other hand, so the level of detail will depend on your roadmap's intended audience.

The risk of an output-focused roadmap often equates to a product team that releases feature after feature, and no tie back to the reason for those features. A *feature factory* is the term often used to describe such teams. You released a bunch of features; the key question becomes: did they achieve the outcome you were seeking?

Timing

When it comes to dates in your roadmap, there is a lot of contention. Many stakeholders are looking to the roadmap to tell them exactly what they can expect and when. However, that type of artifact is not a roadmap—it's a project plan or a release plan. Michael Salerno, VP of Product at Brainshark, puts it simply: "A roadmap is not a release plan. A roadmap is a sequence of stakeholder priorities and requires concept feasibility for delivery. A release plan requires rigorous scope definition and engineering capacity planning."

This still doesn't exempt a roadmap from including timeframes, though; in fact, we listed timeframes as an essential component of product roadmaps in Chapter 2. But as Jim Garretson, Director of Product at Candescent Health, explains, "We don't tie expectations to distant roadmap deadlines. The roadmap has to tell the product story, but it doesn't have to get the days right." So, rather than specific dates and features, we recommend timeframes that are less specific than January 2017, or even Q2 2018.

Loose timeframes like Now, Next, and Later can still satisfy the teams and stakeholders without offering specific delivery dates. Save those specifics for the release and project plans!

We do realize that in some instances your product must be out the door by a certain date; for example, when your software is embedded into another product with strict production deadlines, such as having initial software loaded onto a television. But we still hold that this level of specificity should be at the project or release plan level, and not on the roadmap.

SpaceX

In September 2016, Elon Musk, CEO of SpaceX (and Tesla Motors), announced his roadmap to colonize Mars. His presentation and roadmap overview are a great example of how product vision, strategy, business objectives, and themes all come together.

Product Vision

Let's start with SpaceX's published corporate vision statement:

SpaceX was founded under the belief that a future where humanity is out exploring the stars is fundamentally more exciting than one where we are not. Today SpaceX is actively developing the technologies to make this possible, with the ultimate goal of enabling human life on Mars.

This statement contains elements of vision, mission, and values. The distinctions are not important here; what is important is that Musk outlined an aspiration for the company, a reason why it exists, and a clear statement of how we all will benefit if they succeed.

To make the benefit absolutely clear, he pointed out:

The alternative to an extinction event is to become a multi-planet species.

Using the word *product* somewhat loosely, the first major component of SpaceX's product vision is to "create a self-sustaining city on Mars." Why Mars? Tying directly back to the organization's mission, Elon describes it as: "the best option among nearby planets for a self-sustaining civilization."

Business Objectives

Musk begins his discussion of strategy by outlining the key problem with getting people to Mars: money. He estimates it would currently cost around $10 billion per person. There is therefore "no overlap between people who want to go and people who can afford to." To make emigration to Mars market-viable, SpaceX would have to "drive the cost to the equivalent to a house in the US—about US $200,000." That sounds like a business objective with a built-in key result.

Themes

Musk then asks, for this strategy to be viable, what would need to be true? His team has done the research and defined the themes this way:

- Full spacecraft reusability
- Refueling in orbit
- Propellent production on Mars
- Right propellant

These four themes don't describe the specific technology or solution, but are all subgoals of the affordability objective. Each of these subgoals can also be a theme (we'll discuss subthemes further in Chapter 6) that can become part of the roadmap.

Key Results

The key results for the objectives tied to the first theme of "Full spacecraft reusability" could be:

- The overall market cost is $200,000 or lower.
- The reusability of rocket transportation is 90% or greater.
- Tons of propellant can be produced on Mars.

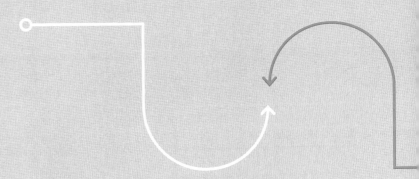

Summary

Guiding principles forming a vision of the future for your customer and your organization, and a strategy for achieving them, are essential ingredients of a compelling roadmap. Framing the timing and deliverables for your product within these buckets will help you establish, explain, and gain alignment on your roadmap.

Splitting the strategy portion of your roadmap into objectives and key results will allow you to direct your product development efforts toward measurable outcomes rather than specific outputs such as features and functions. Focus your measurement efforts on fewer than five objectives that will make the most difference to the success of your customer and organization.

In Chapters 5 and 6 we'll cover how to discover and focus on solving for these key customer needs.

Chapter 5

Uncovering Customer Needs Through Themes

What you'll learn in this chapter

The importance of expressing customer needs

Definitions of themes and subthemes

Ways to uncover themes and subthemes

How to use job stories and user stories to support themes

How to transform needs into themes and subthemes

Ways to relate your themes to objectives

How to handle features in your roadmap

Chapter

5

Uncovering Customer Needs Through Themes

Identifying customer needs is the most important aspect of your roadmapping process.

Roadmaps should be about expressing those customer needs. Therefore, most items on your roadmap will derive from a job the customer needs to accomplish or a problem the customer must solve.

Uncovering those needs can be a challenge in and of itself. On top of that, you must vet every need to make sure your understanding is not biased by your assumptions or warped by your rose-colored glasses. So, in this chapter, we'll go into quite a lot of detail on how to investigate, identify, and define customer needs.

Expressing Customer Needs

In the Preface, we related the product professional to an executive chef, and compared building products to crafting meals. In this metaphor, the roadmap is equivalent to the chef's menu; it defines what will be delivered. But so far we don't have anything on it! Now we get to the real value—figuring out what goes on the menu, in what order, and how it will be presented.

If you've done the groundwork, you will have uncovered a real problem worth solving. In other words, you have identified a "job to be done" that is frustrating and inconvenient enough for a customer to seek out and "hire" a solution to address that discomfort. Additionally, if your guiding principles are properly set, then you also have a clear vision for a desired end state and the goals that will get you there. With those things in place, you're ready to get into the details.

The next step is to extract all of the precise problems or needs that must be addressed in order for your product to add value to the customer. This is a critical component because every decision about your product should be rooted in customer needs. Staying focused here helps you avoid building things your customers don't need, forces you to be efficient, and ultimately ensures that you deliver the highest possible value to your customer base.

Your roadmap helps you match those customer needs with what's important to your business to thrive and grow. It doesn't matter whether you're building an MVP, a version 2, or release #97. We recommend you start by understanding and organizing the most important customer needs first.

As we touched upon earlier, we recommend that you draw a clear distinction between the product roadmap and the release plan (see Figure 5-1). Your roadmap should be a high-level view of *what* needs and problems your product should solve, while also helping you confirm *why*. In contrast, your release plan should detail *how* you will solve them. The product roadmap should not be about developing solutions or defining what your product will look like. Leave that to the release plan!

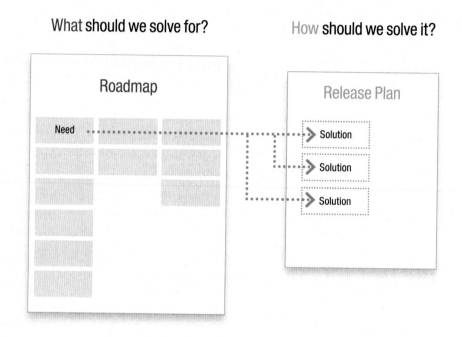

FIGURE 5-1. *A product roadmap versus a release plan*

Themes and Subthemes

As we've touched on, in the relaunched roadmapping process we use *themes* and *subthemes* to express customer needs. This is probably a new concept for many of you, so let's define what we mean by these terms.

Themes are an organizational construct for defining what's important to your customers at the present time.

The difference between themes and subthemes is granularity, or level of detail. A ***theme*** is a high-level customer need. A ***subtheme*** is a more specific need. Themes can stand on their own, but they can also represent a grouping of subthemes. Let's look at a generic software example:

Theme: Address key usability issues
Subtheme: Pagination
Subtheme: Menu navigation
Subtheme: Save status

In this example, you can see the high-level need is to improve usability for the customer. The subthemes then highlight more-granular needs that you can explore to accomplish the larger theme.

Now let's revisit the garden hose example from earlier in the book:

Theme: Indestructibility
Subtheme: No kinks
Subtheme: No leaks

So, again, themes and subthemes represent the needs and problems your product will solve for. A need is generally something the customer doesn't have yet, whereas a problem is something that's not working right (with the existing product, or whatever substitute they might currently be using). Even though these two terms suggest subtle differences, the important point is that both refer to a gap or pain in the customer's experience. When identifying the themes and subthemes for your roadmap, remember to consider both needs and problems from all angles.

Jared Spool, paraphrasing our very own Bruce McCarthy, says, "Themes help teams stay focused without prematurely committing to a solution that may not be the best idea later on."* As Spool points out, it is important to focus most of the roadmapping effort on customer needs and problems because "the viability of a feature may shift dramatically, while the nature of an important customer problem will likely remain the same."

---

*https://medium.com/uie-brain-sparks/themes-a-small-change-to-product-roadmaps-with-large-effects-a9a9a496b800

Organizing roadmaps by theme and subtheme can have a number of distinct advantages. Some of those include:

- Focusing on customer needs helps the team say "no" to unnecessary solutions.

- Focusing on customer needs helps the team shift away from playing competitive catch-up (and instead gain competitive advantage by focusing on what's missing or what nobody else is doing).

- Focusing on customer needs creates a better and more intuitive narrative for sales and marketing.

- A clearly defined need makes solution development easier.

- Starting with customer needs provides development teams with more freedom and flexibility when considering solutions.

- Customer needs are generally smaller in number than a laundry list of features, making the roadmap easier to read and use.

In our experience many product teams fail to hit the mark with their products because "so many features in today's products are solutions without a clear problem to solve."* Their understanding of customer needs or problems is unclear or off-base. One of the reasons we believe themes are so important is because they force you to focus on the need before you even start to consider solutions—and then to evaluate how well each potential solution meets that need. The more rigorous you are about understanding customer needs, the easier it will be to develop the right solutions.

---

*Ibid.

Ways to Uncover Themes and Subthemes

User Journeys and Experience Maps

One great way to begin unpacking customer needs when developing a new product or rethinking an existing one is through a **user journey map**. The journey map is a tool that helps you understand every step a user takes when solving a problem. Beginning with the moment the user realizes the problem exists, the journey then tracks the user's actions through the current methods they employ to address it, and ends when the problem has been solved and the user moves on.

Good user journey maps are usually highly detailed, examining even the most minute actions, movements, and tasks. They help uncover opportunities to improve snags and pain points. These snags and pain points end up being the basis for your themes and subthemes.

If you're looking to learn more about user journeys, we'd highly recommend James Kalbach's book *Mapping Experiences: A Complete Guide to Creating Value Through Journeys, Blueprints, and Diagrams* (O'Reilly).

Figure 5-2 shows an example of a vacation traveler's user journey. This is a very simple example, but here you can see we've identified high-level phases in the journey and then defined the more detailed steps in each phase the user will take when planning to travel.

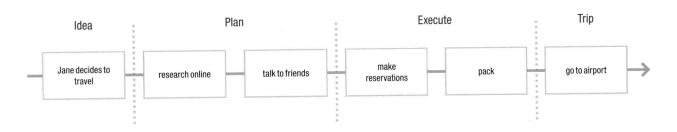

FIGURE 5-2. *A vacation traveler's user journey*

At times it can be helpful to go a level deeper on the user journey maps by plotting all of them together into an ***experience map*** (Figure 5-3). Experience maps show how customer actions relate across customer types and phases, and can also be used to tease out other dimensions like emotions, technology needs, and more. We create experience maps when we want to understand how everything fits together. They also help validate which points and opportunities are most important.

Jim Kalbach's book, mentioned earlier, is a fantastic source for understanding how to properly explore, understand, and map journeys and experiences.

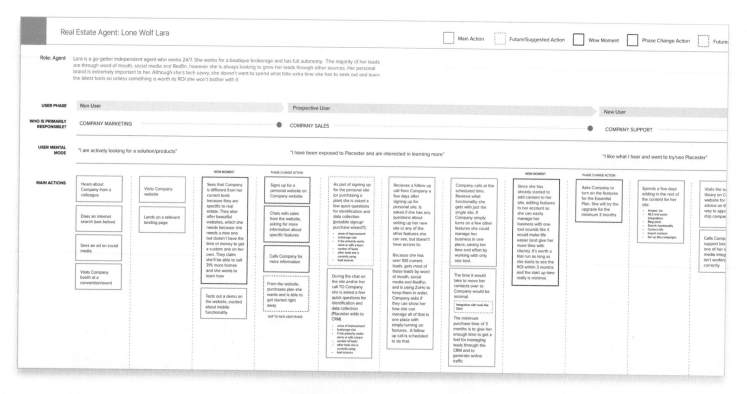

FIGURE 5-3. *A user experience map*

To bring the concept of journey mapping into more focus, let's consider another example of a product that you may be familiar with: the popular ride-sharing startup Lyft. It's fair to assume that one of the initial problems that Lyft set out to address was that in a hectic urban environment, it was generally hard to find a taxi (in addition, of course, to other taxi-related problems, like not accepting credit cards, dirty cabs, unpredictable fares, etc.). To competently solve this problem, the product team at Lyft needed to understand all of the incremental steps in the urban traveler's experience. To do so, they might have created a map of the journey the user takes to resolve the problem.

In the case of Lyft, the customer's journey usually starts with a need to go from point A to point B. Some steps in the journey might look like this, in order of experience:

1. Search for travel options.
2. Decide which travel method to use.
3. Employ chosen travel method.
4. Board the travel mechanism.
5. Travel from point A to point B (aka transit).

…and so on until the individual has reached the destination and moved on with their day.

The visual metaphor we like to use for the journey map is crossing a fast-moving stream. Imagine for a second your user is standing on one side of a rushing stream, trying to figure out how to cross without falling in. In order to do so, they need to choose which rocks they will step on, in what order, to land on the other side safely. Not only that, they'll want to pick the easiest and most efficient path. In this metaphor, you can think of the stream as representing the user's "problem" and the rocks as the steps in their journey toward solving that problem.

The steps in the journey map give you zones you can zoom into to understand the user at a deeper level. With this understanding, you can start to define each need or job in more detail. Those needs go on your roadmap as themes and subthemes.

Existing Product Needs

If your product team is working on an existing product, you may already have a good understanding of user journeys. Or then again, do you? How long has it been since you sketched out a user journey map? Have you ever gone a step further and created an experience map? In dealing with lists of feature requests and stakeholder demands, we sometimes forget to be discerning. In other words, many product people fall into the trap of accepting those requests at face value instead of asking the right questions, like "Why does this matter?" or "What need or problem does it solve?" or "How does it make the customer's life easier?" or "Is there a bigger problem that needs solving?"

With existing products, it can be easy to operate on autopilot, especially when you're in a rhythm of collecting and prioritizing feedback. Maybe we get overconfident from years of working on the same product with the same customer base, or maybe we simply get lazy. Regardless, the key is to focus on understanding "why" a need or problem is worth solving (or not). The user journey map is a great way to do this because it provides context.

(Job stories and user stories also help ferret out "why," which we'll discuss a bit later in the chapter.) When you get a request for a feature, you can employ the user journey map to make sense of where that need fits into the context of the user experience. Is it a critical path item, or simply nice to have? Is the existence of the unsolved need or problem impeding the user's journey in a significant way?

Teams working on stable existing products likely won't need to create the user journey from scratch, but you can certainly benefit from returning to it to cross-reference how a request or demand fits into the experience. Once you understand how and where the customer experiences the need, you can work directly with them to validate the problem and test possible solutions. Returning to your user journey maps on a regular basis will also ensure they stay up-to-date. As human beings we constantly evolve and change, which means your understanding of your customer's journey may already be out-of-date!

System Needs

So far we've talked about the concept of themes and subthemes in the context of customer needs. The reason for this, of course, is that your product exists to improve the life of the customer! However, not every need will come from your customer. You must also consider "system" or infrastructure needs. There are layers of functionality and operational tooling that need to be built into the backend or framework of your technology in order to make it work. You need to account for these critical items on your roadmap as well. Some product professionals differentiate between these two types of needs by calling them *functional* needs (customer-focused) versus *technical* or *nonfunctional* needs (engineering-focused). If it helps, you can think of your system as a special sort of customer.

To use another metaphor, we can compare building a product to constructing a home. The infrastructure or backend of a product is akin to the foundation, framing, rough plumbing, and electrical of a house. These forms and systems tie everything together and make the house functional. The flooring, windows, furniture, and other finishes are equivalent to the frontend layer that the customer sees and interacts with. Again, most of our discussion around themes to this point has been related to customer needs, because that's who you're serving. However, the infrastructure also has to be in place in order for the tool to actually function.

Let's consider a simple example. In 2014, Evan's product development firm built a mobile physical therapy application. The product was designed to replace the traditional one-page paper handouts that most physical therapists assign as homework for patients in between visits. These handouts are typically cartoon drawings of exercises with short, and often insufficient, text descriptions.

There are a number of problems with these handouts. Most commonly, patients misplace them and thus forget how to do the exercises or lose motivation altogether. No exercises, no healing. To address this problem, Evan's company developed an interactive mobile tool with exercise videos, progress tracking, and a direct line of communication to the PT.

After the initial release, many client facilities wanted to address the need for patients to pay for services directly in the app. This customer need was added to the roadmap as:

Theme: Billing & payments

However, this theme required backend or system-level integration. Therefore, a few technical subthemes were included:

Subtheme: Billing & payments API integration
Subtheme: API integration testing

So while your roadmap should first and foremost be focused on customer needs, make sure you consider the infrastructure needs as well.

Opportunity-Solution Trees

Many teams generate a lot of ideas when they go through a journey-mapping or experience-mapping exercise. There are so many opportunities for improving things for the customer that they quickly become overwhelmed by a mass of problems, solutions, needs, and ideas without much structure or priority. We'll cover prioritization techniques in detail in Chapter 7, but it's first helpful to organize the information you have into a manageable framework.

Teresa Torres, Product Discovery Coach, Product Talk*, has developed a visualization for this problem that she says has revolutionized the way teams make decisions. She calls them Opportunity-Solution Trees and we've found them a brilliant way to distinguish solutions from the problem, need, or other opportunity they are intended to address—while at the same time tying them together logically.

Teresa says it all starts with a clear desired outcome. Remember those business objectives from Chapter 4: examples such as increasing your conversion rate or customer engagement? Those. (Hopefully you can see where this is going.) What Teresa calls opportunities, we call themes. We share the nomenclature of solutions and experiments designed to validate those solutions.

This hierarchy, similar to what we advocate in this book, simplifies decision-making by separating decisions among objectives, themes, and solutions. Each decision is a comparison among a small number of like things. Working down this hierarchy, level-by-level, allows teams narrow their testing and development efforts to solving one problem at a time.

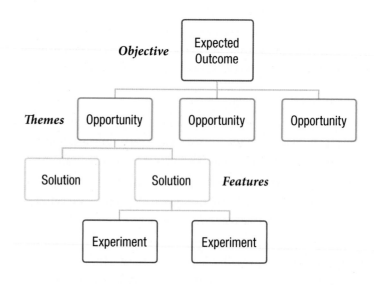

FIGURE 5-4. *A concept of the Opportunity-Solution Tree*

---

*For more about the Opportunity Solution Tree see Teresa Torres' blog: *https://www.producttalk.org/opportunity-solution-tree*

Imagine, for example, that you are a sea captain in the 1500s and you have an objective to cross the Atlantic Ocean. You may encounter certain problems along the way such as scurvy or pirates. Preventing these problems become your themes. If scurvy becomes an immediate problem (because some of the crew are already suffering), you will begin to generate solutions such as feeding them oranges or grapefruit. Feeding them apples might also seem like a good idea in general, but since only citrus fruits contain the necessary vitamin C, apples do not solve the problem at hand and should be set aside. (See? This is why you should never compare apples and oranges!)

If the objective is a healthy crew, the themes in this example would emerge as: Healthy Diet, Regular Exercise, and Ship Cleanliness. Fruit is a solution (i.e., feature) and the experiment between Apples and Oranges could determine which crewmembers get healthy quicker.

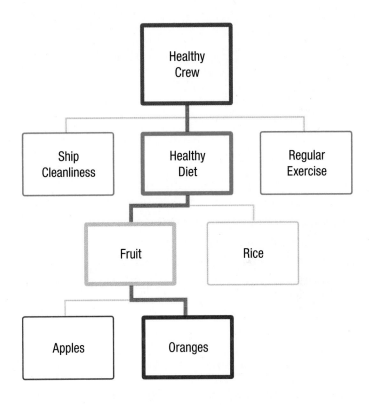

FIGURE 5-5. *An example of the Opportunity-Solution Tree*

Using Job Stories and User Stories to Support Themes

Describing customer needs without getting into the solution can be tricky business. To make it easier, many product teams use a framework to tease out the reasons behind a need and justify its importance. The purpose is to prevent assumptions and avoid building things that don't match the real needs of the customer. The two most common forms of this method are called **user stories** (from Agile software development) and **job stories** (from the jobs-to-be-done framework).

The format for *user stories* is typically:

> **As a** [*user type*]
> **I want** [*desire*]
> **So I can** [*result*]

The generally accepted format for a *job story* is:

> **When** [*situation/motivation*]
> **I need** [*desire*]
> **So I can** [*result*]

In each of these frameworks, the focus is on the customer, what they want or need, and (critically) *why* that's important to them. Themes work in the same way but at a higher level, and we've developed a similar (but 33% simpler!) framework for expressing themes.

The format for themes is:

> **Ensure** [*result*] for [*stakeholder*]

Some examples:

- Make mobile experience as good as desktop for users.

- Make sharing via social networks fun and easy for users.

- Ensure access during peak times for users.

If you're familiar with Agile methodologies, this will feel familiar—and that's very deliberate. Just as Agile epics break down into their constituent user stories, we use user stories or job stories to support themes as well. The point is to make sure we answer *why* each theme is relevant or important before committing to it.

Let's use the Lyft example again to look at how these concepts can all fit together.

Term	Definition	Example
Theme	A high-level customer or system need.	Avoid surprises for customers
Job story	A motivation focused story about the customer that provides as much context as possible on a specific customer need.[1]	When a user has to travel across town for a last-minute meeting She needs to quickly determine how fast she can get there So she can decide if this mode of transport is her best option for on-time arrival

TABLE 5-1. *How a theme can be broken down into a job-story*

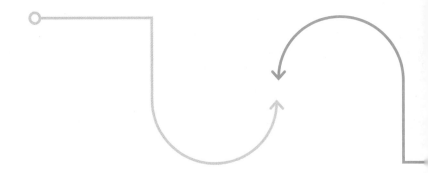

Themes Are About Outcomes, Not Outputs

Many product people are used to filling roadmaps with features and solutions, and we can attest from experience that old habits die hard. The key question to ask yourself when faced with a list of concrete deliverables is why? Why are these things important? What will result from doing them? How will the fortunes of the company or the happiness of the customer improve? Why would we do this at all?

By asking yourself (or whomever is requesting a particular feature) why, you are attempting to discern the difference between the output requested and the result or outcome desired. In other words, you are attempting to distinguish the end from the means. Recall our discussion about output versus outcome from Chapter 4 in regards to objectives and key results. This is making a similar point, but in the context of themes. Table 5-2 gives some examples you can use to help you translate ideas for solutions into themes.

Notice that translating proposed outputs into themes leaves open the possibility there may be other—even better—ways to achieve the same outcomes. Maybe instead of an HTML5 redesign of the whole site, certain core functions mobile users like to perform on the go could be ported into a native iOS or Android app. That might be less work and more effective in achieving the result described in the theme.

Output	Why?	Theme (Outcome)
HTML5 redesign	Works better on mobile	Make mobile experience as good as desktop
Twitter and Facebook integration	Allows customers to promote the product by sharing results	Make it easy and fun for users to promote our product
Infrastructure work for scalability	App slows down under heavy traffic	Ensure access and that we can fulfill peak demand

TABLE 5-2. *How to transform outputs (solutions) into outcomes (themes)*

Relating Themes Back to Your Objectives

Now that you've identified needs and translated them into themes, your roadmap is starting to take shape and become useful. Before moving on, though, you must tie the themes on your roadmap back to your strategic objectives. This step is incredibly important because it helps you stay focused on the right things and avoid distraction. Let's take a second to review the product roadmapping hierarchy again:

I. Product vision
The problem you're solving, or the change you want to see in the world

II. Objectives
The high-level goals you want to accomplish in this next version of the product

III. Themes and subthemes
The customer needs or problems that you are addressing

What you're striving for is to ensure that every step in the roadmapping process is incremental and builds on the one before it. Remember, your roadmap is the foundation or blueprint for what you're building, so it first and foremost needs to answer the *why*. Each element informs and feeds into the next. Your objectives help you realize your product vision, and your themes and subthemes help you accomplish your objectives.

So, with your strategic objectives clearly defined and approved by all stakeholders, the next step is to make sure that every theme on your roadmap relates directly to your objectives. Look at each theme or subtheme critically with your team. It's possible for a theme to link to more than one objective, and that's fine. In fact, it's great if a theme can inform multiple goals.

One good way to link themes to objectives is to color-code your objectives, and then tag themes with the associated color. Figure 5-4 shows an example of such a "theme card." On the card, we've included a section at the top identifying the business objective the theme relates to. As you can see, the color-coded orange bar references Objective 3.

The theme card is only one possible approach. There are other ways to present this, but we've found this to be useful.

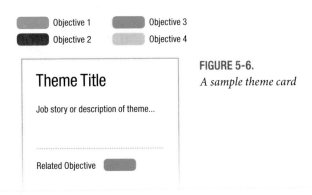

FIGURE 5-6.
A sample theme card

Let's think again about the SpaceX example from Chapter 4 and above. If one of the themes on the SpaceX team's roadmap is "refuel in orbit," we can link that to the objective "reduce the cost of space travel to what an average American family can afford." Here we imagine that refueling in orbit is an efficiency-related priority, which, if executed successfully, should help lower the cost of travel. Figure 5-5 shows what that might look like in another version of the card format.

If any theme on your roadmap does not map back to an objective, this should be a warning sign. This is an incredibly important point, so we'll say it again: every theme on your roadmap should relate to at least one of your strategic objectives! If you have trouble connecting a theme back to an objective, take the time to review the theme in question with your team to determine if it should be part of your roadmap at all. It may be that it simply needs to be reframed or reworded. Or maybe it needs to be moved to another column in your roadmap to be reconsidered in the next round.

As a final note, we want to stress that every time you plan a big update to your roadmap, you should review and reconsider your objectives. For example, when you're ready to move things from the Next column to the Now column, or from the Later column to the Next column, this is a good time to reconsider your objectives. The reason is that as time passes, your strategic objectives will change. Your business or product may be making a transition, rendering some of your objectives obsolete. Or maybe some of your objectives have been adequately addressed for now and you want to prioritize other things. Regardless, each new version of your roadmap should start with revisiting your product vision and strategic objectives. Linking themes to objectives will then ensure you're moving in the right direction and will increase the chances of your product adding real value—to your business, your customers, your technology, or all of the above.

Refuel in Orbit

When a space vehicle is traveling to or from Mars, **it needs to** refuel in orbit, **to** limit the amount of fuel needed on board and prevent delays.

Related Objective:
Reduce the cost of space travel to what an average American family can afford

FIGURE 5-7.
Using a theme card to link a SpaceX theme to one of its objectives

Real-World Themes

The High Cost of Space Travel

In his roadmap to Mars, which we covered in Chapter 4's case study, Elon Musk identified the core problem preventing people from emigrating to Mars: *cost*. His roadmap for developing a lower-cost interplanetary transportation system had to reduce the cost of going to Mars by 5 million percent. That sounds crazy, and the SpaceX team has not yet developed the technologies to make it work, but at the time of announcing this roadmap, they had worked out what would be *necessary* to make it work. The themes, then, of Musk's roadmap are these four problems they need to solve:

- Full reusability

- Refueling in orbit

- Propellant production on Mars

- Right propellant

Fun as it is to think about interplanetary homesteading, let's take a look at how themes work in more terrestrial product roadmaps.

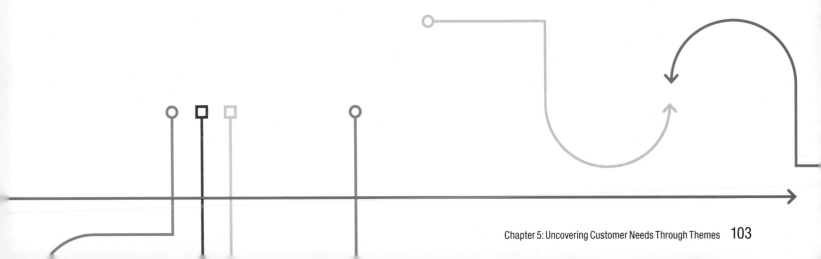

Slack's Theme-based Roadmap

The popular messaging platform Slack recently followed many others in publishing a public roadmap via Trello, as shown in Figure 5-6.

Details on anything not yet released are thin, and the names and descriptions of individual items are chosen with the goal in mind, rather than the specific deliverable. Items like "Streamlined app development" and "Deeper integration points" provide the team leeway in determining the best solution and design for tackling each problem. (Some others are more specific, including "Advanced link previews.")

What best communicates where Slack is focused, however, is the "About this roadmap" card, where they say the roadmap "describes our platform development plans for the benefit of developers creating tools that interact with Slack."

They then add: "There are three major themes in our platform roadmap that we want to highlight," including app discovery, interactivity, and developer experience. They cover a little about the goals of each, with explanations like "we're doing more to help customers discover the right apps and engage with the apps they've already installed." Each roadmap item is then tagged with one or more of these themes to indicate why it is important to their chosen customer, the app developer.

With very few details, Slack's roadmap effectively communicates who they serve, what their priorities are and why, and just enough details about what's in the hopper to make people confident in their direction.

They can do this because they know who their customer is and what they expect. As product executive and strategist Sarela Bliman-Cohen explains, "In order to have a good roadmap, you need to look at the markets you're after. You need to identify the ones where you can succeed. Once you understand the markets you're after, then you can have a thematic roadmap."

FIGURE 5-8. *Slack's public roadmap on Trello*

GOV.uk's Gantt Chart with Benefits

GOV.uk provides an online service to help UK citizens find government services and information. Their 2016–2017 roadmap, published in *ProductPlan*, does a good job of organizing a lot of detail into themes, as shown in Figure 5-7.

Each of the major white sections describes a long-term theme such as "Make it possible to join content together as services," and contains a few subthemes, like "Improve tagging, navigation, search, and notification systems." This is clearly an attempt to get more specific and describe the value of their planned work in a way that might be understood by outsiders (though it does still contain some tech jargon).

If you click on one of those subthemes, it expands to show you the phases of work going on to support that objective (see Figure 5-8). Many of these ("Discovery on moving to PaaS," "Alpha on moving to PaaS," "Move 1st frontend apps") may be cryptic to the average citizen, but you get a sense of things progressing, and we applaud the attempt at transparency. These additional details provide a sense of status for each item, which is a very helpful component to add to the roadmap. We talk more about this in Chapter 6.

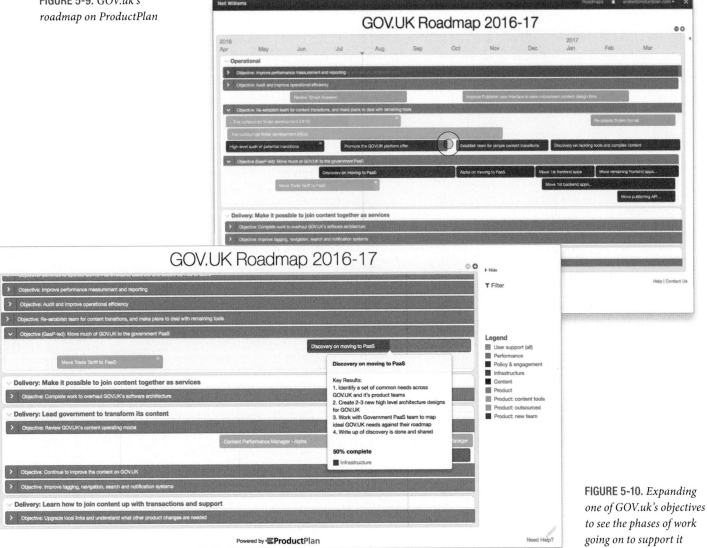

FIGURE 5-9. *GOV.uk's roadmap on ProductPlan*

FIGURE 5-10. *Expanding one of GOV.uk's objectives to see the phases of work going on to support it*

Themes are customer needs.

Not features.

Summary

Uncovering user needs is an incredibly important part of product roadmapping because your product exists to make the customer's life better. Thus, most of the items on the roadmap should be focused on serving the customer.

User journey maps can be used to outline a user's path through the problem space. A close inspection of those maps will help you clarify the customer's needs. Once you've validated the needs, you can add them to your roadmap as key themes or subthemes to address. Those themes and subthemes can then be vetted and supported by job stories or user stories. Buttressing your themes with job stories helps you cross-check and validate their importance to the customer and the value in solving for them. Finally, make sure every theme or subtheme on your roadmap is linked to a strategic objective and contributes to the overall goals of your product.

One key point we'd like to reiterate: stick to needs when defining themes and subthemes. You will be very tempted, believe us, to start brainstorming solutions or sketching ideas. Avoid this temptation! Stay focused on the needs at this stage. Defining solutions will come next, and developing them will be a whole lot more fun and effective when you're confident about why they need to be implemented.

Footnotes

1 *https://jtbd.info/replacing-the-user-story-with-the-job-story-af7cdee10c27*

Chapter 6

Deepening Your Roadmap

What you'll learn in this chapter

How themes and features can work together

Using stage of development

How to communicate confidence

Identifying target customers

Chapter

6

Deepening Your Roadmap

A little context helps you spend less time explaining the roadmap and more time executing it.

Secondary components can help you spend less time explaining each item on the roadmap.

In Chapter 2, we identified primary and secondary components of a product roadmap, and some complementary information you may want to consider to provide context. Up to this point, we have focused primarily on the primary ones, including:

- Product vision
- Business objectives
- Themes
- Timeframes
- Disclaimer

In this chapter, we want to sketch out how the additional details provided by the following secondary components can increase clarity, readability, and value for stakeholders:

- Features and solutions
- Stage of development
- Confidence
- Target customers
- Product areas

Although we consider these additional components "secondary" because the roadmap is still valuable without them, the level of detail they add makes it easier to communicate, helping immensely with buy-in and alignment. This means you'll spend less time explaining the roadmap and more time executing it. See Chapter 9 for guidelines about putting together the right mix of these components depending on your audience.

Additionally, the added detail will help you think more critically about each item on the roadmap. As we touched upon in Chapter 5, many product people fall into the trap of incorporating features into the roadmap based on instinct or stakeholder demand. This common misstep often leads to building the wrong things and sending the product off-course. Instead, the components we cover in this chapter will encourage your team to keep asking "why" at every juncture and help you stress-test each item on your roadmap.

Features and Solutions: How They Can Work with Themes

If themes represent the customer's most important needs or problems to be solved, then features (or solutions) are what you plan to build or implement in order to help users manage them. Even though we advocate focusing on customer needs during roadmapping, it is sometimes appropriate to account for certain solutions on the roadmap as well. In this section, we tackle how themes and features can be combined successfully.

When and Why Do Features Appear on the Roadmap?

Even if you commit fully to the theme-based roadmap concept, you may find it impossible to avoid including certain features or solutions. This is common, and we see a few repeat patterns for when and why this happens. The three scenarios presented next outline common reasons why solutions make their way onto a theme-based roadmap. Even though we try to avoid it, we don't shy away from it when it's necessary. There are other reasons of course, but we're focusing here on the three we've seen most consistently.

Probable solutions

First, some teams decide to include "probable" solutions on the roadmap. This doesn't mean the team has decided on a final solution, but instead that a likely solution is evident. Listing a likely solution does not remove the need for testing and validation, but it can at times provide a helpful starting point for exploration.

Let's revisit the example of Evan's mobile physical therapy application from the previous chapter. You might recall that the team included a theme on the roadmap called "Billing & payments." In addition to the technical subthemes mentioned in Chapter 5, the team also identified other subthemes, including:

Subtheme: Distribute invoices
Subtheme: Track status

Acknowledging these needs, the team decided QuickBooks was a probable solution for these needs. Even though this option was not fully vetted or validated, the team had enough confidence based on previous work to include it on the roadmap as a likely solution.

Infrastructure solutions

Second, infrastructure solutions often appear on a roadmap. Remember from Chapter 5 that your roadmap not only will include customer needs, but will also take into consideration your underlying technology. Often infrastructure needs are defined and vetted internally by the engineering team, and usually require less validation from stakeholders and external audiences. When it comes to protocols and tools for function and optimization, we trust our engineers to make sound decisions. It is therefore often the case that system-level needs transition into solutions very quickly.

For example, we might include a very specific solution related to search, such as "Solr Proof of Concept." The team knows they want to use Solr for the underlying search engine, so they're comfortable listing that as a subtheme on the roadmap. If you have validated your solution, it's OK to be explicit about this on the roadmap.

Carryover solutions

A third common scenario relates to carryover. It is often the case that something from a previous roadmap or release plan gets pushed to the next iteration, generally because the team ran out of time or resources to execute on it. We call these *carryover* themes or features. If we were unable to ship something from a previous plan, we can include that item as a subtheme on our next version of the roadmap.

As we discussed in Chapters 1 and 2, it is almost impossible for product teams to predict with exact accuracy when something is going to be complete, so carryover is common.

Where Do Features Appear on the Roadmap?

When adding features to a roadmap, it's important to retain the context of why they are there. We don't want solutions to replace themes on the roadmap, and we don't list features and themes side by side. Instead, we recommend adding features as subthemes so it is clear what problem they are intended to solve. As a reminder, subthemes are more specific needs, and generally provide more detail about the need expressed in the higher-level theme.

In Figure 6-1, which uses the physical therapy example again, you can see the product team has included three subthemes. The first two are need-based, but the third clearly defines PayPal as a probable solution. As this example shows, subthemes can be need-based, but they are also a great way to capture known or probable solutions when appropriate.

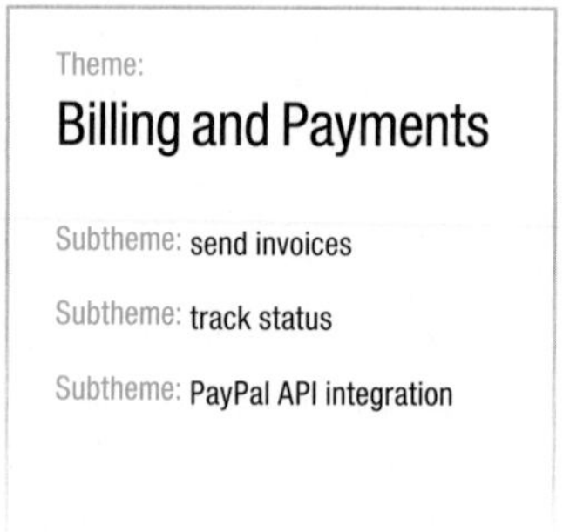

Theme:
Billing and Payments

Subtheme: send invoices

Subtheme: track status

Subtheme: PayPal API integration

FIGURE 6-1. *Subthemes can relate to both needs and probable or known solutions*

Buffer's feature-level roadmap

Buffer, the social media sharing tool, has taken sharing to new levels, publishing information on revenue, salaries, diversity, and, as of recently, their product roadmap, shown in Figure 6-2. Like the Slack example we showed earlier in the book, Buffer is using Trello to communicate what it is working on (or planning to). Here, the individual items are very specific as to the deliverable planned. Labels like "Pause Button" and "Allow multiple admins for Business customers" leave little room for discovery or experimentation and do not describe the problem to be solved, job to be done, or value to the user.

Buffer takes transparency far here, allowing customers to comment and even vote on individual features (Figure 6-3). Buffer also solicits feature requests, which can be viewed, commented on, and voted on in turn.

Many product people are rightfully wary about sharing this level of detail with customers, as are we. Early in the process—when specifics are not certain—problems, needs, jobs to be done, or other ways of framing the theme of the effort are usually sufficient.

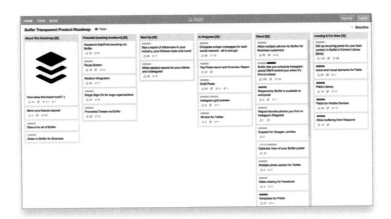

FIGURE 6-2. *Buffer's public roadmap on Trello*

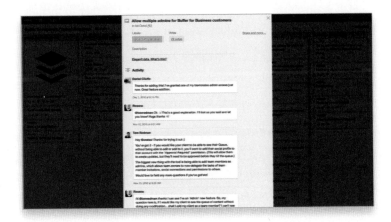

FIGURE 6-3. *Buffer allows customers to view, comment, and vote on individual features*

Feature questions

When considering whether to add features to your roadmap, ask yourself these questions:

- Do we have enough understanding of the need and possible solutions to feel confident in a particular solution?

- Do we have any validated solutions from previous release plans that did not get completed and need to be carried over?

- Do we have any validated infrastructure needs?

- Do we have any mandates from decision-making stakeholders that must be addressed?

- What is the likelihood that this solution will be changed, postponed, or dropped form the schedule (i.e., what is your confidence)?

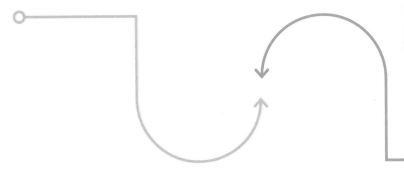

Using Stage of Development

Before being released to the public, products generally pass through several steps in the development process. Different industries and individual organizations use their own terms, but commonly there is a *discovery*, *market research*, or *R&D* stage before stages like *design*, *testing*, or *prototyping*. These are then followed by stages with names like *development* or *pre-production*. In the software business, there are often stages approaching a first general release called *alpha* and *beta* or *early access*, where a limited set of customers test the product to provide feedback. Labels like this clearly convey to the team and stakeholders where we stand on solving for each need. In early 2017, Evan and C. Todd worked with the Spotify product team to identify opportunities for improvement in their road-mapping process. During that workshop, one of Spotify's lead product managers shared a version of her roadmap. On the roadmap she'd tagged each item as either "think it," "ship it," or "tweak it." In this simple way, her team was able to indicate the stage of each item on the roadmap to all stakeholders. When a stakeholder sees an item labeled "think it," they know the theme is still being considered or explored.

Another interesting insight about the Spotify example is that status labels also help differentiate between themes and features. Any item labeled "think it" has clearly not been solved for yet, and therefore by definition is a theme. Any item labeled "ship it" or "tweak it" means that a solution has been chosen, and can therefore be considered a feature. This is a great example of how a team might use status to provide additional context to the roadmap.

Stage of Development Questions

Ask yourself these questions when deciding whether to include stage of development information in your roadmap:

- Do your themes or features go through distinct stages of development?

- If so, do those stages take longer than the timeframes in your roadmap?

- Is this level of detail helpful in managing expectations with your stakeholders? (Consider whether confidence, described next, may be sufficient.)

Communicating Confidence

In order to be 100% confident in our ability to execute on a roadmap item—or that a particular item will still be a priority months from now—we'd have to be able to predict the future. Since no one we know possesses that power, we'll go out on a limb and say you should never have 100% confidence in anything on your roadmap. By nature, the roadmap is a strategy tool that outlines what we think is important to our stakeholders. Yes, that information is generally vetted and validated before it hits the roadmap, but there's no way for us to be 100% about any of it.

To a certain extent, the timeframe columns on your roadmap will indicate, at a high level, your confidence in your ability to tackle each theme. Generally, confidence is strongest for items in the nearest column, and wanes the further out you go on the roadmap.

However, even with the implied confidence inherent in roadmap columns, we often add a confidence score to each column as well. For example, we might attach a 75% confidence to the Now column, 50% confidence to the Next column, and 25% confidence to the Later column. These confidence percentages represent our level of certainty that we will deliver on those items in those timeframes.

Predictive Index uses something like this—in its case a decreasing gradient bar—in its roadmap to make it clear that certainty about the contents of the roadmap drops as timeframes become more distant (Figure 6-4).

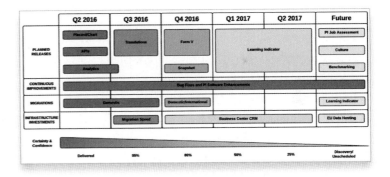

FIGURE 6-4. *Predictive Index uses a decreasing gradient bar to indicate that confidence drops as timeframes grow more distant*

Some product people like to include confidence estimations on individual themes and subthemes. If the additional granularity on each item is helpful for your team, adding confidence to each item on the roadmap can be valuable as well. We've seen this work best when a column represents a general "confidence threshold." For example, if our Now column represents a 70%–95% confidence estimate, then each item can have its own confidence number within that range:

NOW (70%–95%)
- Theme 1: 95%
- Theme 2: 85%
- Theme 3: 80%
- Theme 4: 70%

Finally, some product teams like to include a confidence separation line in their Now column (Figure 6-5). The idea here is that the team is confident in their ability to address anything above the line in the next release. Anything below the line is aspirational. If they get to it, great—bonus points! If not, no harm done. The team can simply move (carry over) the items they miss to the next column or version of the roadmap.

Confidence Questions

Ask yourself these questions when deciding whether to include confidence information in your roadmap:

- Does your roadmap include specific timeframes—e.g., months, quarters, or years?

- Does your roadmap show themes or features far enough into the future that you find yourself reluctant to commit to those items?

- How regularly does your development team hit dates projected months in advance?

- Do your stakeholders tend to assume that if it's written down, it is a promise?

- Have you already included stage-of-development information that might provide enough insight into confidence?

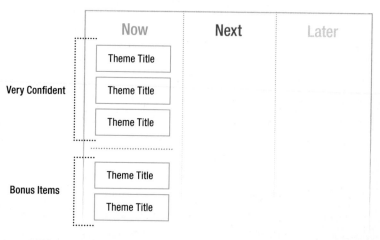

FIGURE 6-5. *How a confidence separation line might appear on a roadmap*

Identifying Target Customers

Many times a product serves more than one customer type. For example, if you set out to solve a problem in the education space, your product might consider the student, teacher, administrator, and even the parent. In addition, your product's users might be different from the actual buyer. If you have to solve for multiple customer types in order for your product to be valuable, then it's a good idea to identify which themes or features apply to which customer types.

On the roadmap this can be as simple as tagging or labeling each theme by the relevant customer type (see Figure 6-6). Other teams create rows in the grid of their roadmap, or swim lanes, for each type of user to create a clearer separation.

When identifying customer needs, it's important to consider *all* of the roles or personas (recall these terms from Chapter 3) your product will solve for. Forcing your team to tag each theme by customer type can help ensure you're focusing on the right customers at the right time.

Target Customers Questions

Ask yourself these questions when deciding whether to include target customers in your roadmap:

- Do you have distinct customer types with different needs?

- Is it important to achieve balance in addressing the needs of each?

- Conversely, are there one or two customer types that are more important?

- Will clarifying the customer type be helpful in guiding stakeholder conversations?

FIGURE 6-6. *Specifying the relevant customer/user for your product*

Tagging Product Areas

Similarly, it can be helpful in ensuring you've covered the essential functionality required by your product to annotate the items on the roadmap by area within the product. A software product might have areas such as user interface, platform, administration, and APIs. A product like our garden hose might have weather surface, exoskeleton, water channel, and connectors.

Each may have separate sets of details such as stage of development, but more important, each must receive sufficient attention on the roadmap to come together into a fully functioning product that meets customer needs. Each may also have separate business objectives.

Product areas can be labeled on themes and features in a similar fashion to target customers or stage of development by using color coding, text labels, or separate rows on the roadmap. Be careful of information overload, though, and consider which of these labels is most important to your stakeholders! (Chapter 9 contains guidance on which stakeholders care most about what information.)

Product Areas Questions

Ask yourself these questions when deciding whether to include product areas in your roadmap:

- Does your product have distinct areas or components that are easy to communicate?

- Do you have separate business objectives for individual product areas?

- Is it important to show that work is being done to improve all areas (or specific areas that need attention most)?

- Will clearly marking product areas be helpful in guiding stakeholder conversations?

Strive for Balance

The optional components we've just outlined are pieces of supplementary information you can add to the roadmap to strengthen the content and make it more useful for your stakeholder audiences.

We have found each of these components to be valuable, but we encourage you to experiment. Which components you use will depend on your unique team, product, and ecosystem. Try incorporating the different components to test out which ones are most useful for your team. It may be that some components are useful for certain times in the product life cycle, while others are not. Experimenting with what information to include on the roadmap may even help you identify other valuable components we have not considered here!

Remember, though, when adding detail to your roadmap, you want to find balance. Too much information can make your roadmap difficult to read or tedious to interact with. However, too little detail can leave a roadmap full of holes, causing confusion and a loss of stakeholder confidence. When this happens, you can expect those stakeholders to come knocking on your door with laundry lists of questions and concerns.

We've found that a selection of these additional components provides a good balance of not too much and not too little. These elements go a long way in justifying decisions and keeping all parties properly informed. A scrutinized and well-organized roadmap leads to improved communication, increased confidence across the team, and, ultimately, better products.

Summary

You learned in this chapter when to incorporate solutions or features into the theme-based roadmap described in Chapter 5. Even though we like to keep the roadmap at the needs level, we acknowledge that features and solutions sometimes need to be included. Generally, we do this by adding them as subthemes to ensure the *why* is retained in the roadmap.

We also spoke about tagging items on your roadmap with additional information such as stage of development, confidence, target customers, and product areas. This additional detail forces you look critically at each item, and provide your stakeholders with enough context to answer their questions and assuage their concerns. The more work you do up front to clarify these details, the easier it will be to communicate with your stakeholders and gain buy-in.

The next step is to start prioritizing to make sure you're addressing everything in the right order. Chapter 7 will walk you through this, so let's get into it!

Chapter 7

Prioritizing—with Science!

What you'll learn in this chapter

Why prioritization is crucial

Bad (but common) ways to prioritize

Five prioritization frameworks

Limitations of using a scoring approach to product decisions

Chapter

7

Prioritizing— with Science!

Wouldn't it be great if no one could argue with your decisions?

In this chapter, we will detail five prioritization frameworks you can use and why you might choose each.

Leveraging an objective and collaborative prioritization method will help stakeholders focus on what's important and come to alignment. It will help you get the buy-in you need to put together a product roadmap that inspires. If it were any more scientific, you'd need a lab coat.

Brenda rushed over from her desk in the sales pit. She was clearly excited. She'd uncovered an opportunity to partner with a local firm that would distribute the company's free demo to a few thousand of their customers, and she was convinced it would be an easy way to generate a lot of new business quickly. Printing demo discs was cheap, so she just wanted my OK to get some cobranded materials made to package them with, and maybe we could do a seminar together and dedicate some telesales resources to following up on the leads. It was nearly free marketing, right?

I said no. I also helped Brenda understand why this didn't fit with our strategy, and where she could more profitably focus her sales efforts. The company had been using a free demo disc for a couple of years to bring in small business customers. We'd run the numbers and it wasn't a highly profitable go-to-market approach. We weren't ready to phase out the SMB business altogether, but it was clear we needed to go up-market.

I redirected Brenda's efforts that day (and for the next year) by sitting down with her and showing her our prioritized list of initiatives and—this is the important part—the underlying strategic goals that informed it. Everything on the list was ranked as to how much we estimated it would help with those goals versus how much effort we estimated it would take.

I put her idea through this model and, although the effort was small, it didn't contribute to our new strategic goal of capturing larger customers, it would probably hurt our conversion rate, and it was unlikely to make much of a dent in our overall revenue picture. Brenda seemed happy to be heard, but being a smart salesperson she also absorbed the changed goals of the company and refocused her prospecting efforts.

A year later, Brenda became our first national accounts salesperson and the highest-paid person in the company. Our move toward larger customers doubled the company's revenue and improved the company's eventual acquisition price not long after.

—Bruce McCarthy, 2010

Why Prioritization Is Crucial

Opportunity Cost

In Bruce's case study, why couldn't the company move up to larger customers and also pursue the small ones with Brenda's low-cost idea? The answer lies in opportunity cost or the fact that, to paraphrase Milton Friedman (and Robert Heinlein), *there's no such thing as a free demo.*

Long experience has taught us that you can never get everything done you would like or even might think is minimally required. Resources are limited, priorities shift, executives have ADHD, and on and on. So if you are not going to get it all done, you have to be very sure you get the *most important* things done before something changes and your resources are redirected. If you are not doing the most important things right now, you risk not having the opportunity to do them in the future.

In fact, this concept is so important to prioritization and road-mapping, that we've developed a rule—nay, a law—to reinforce it:

Always assume you may have to stop work at any time.

This law is a core tenet of the Lean Startup movement popularized by Eric Reis. In his book *The Lean Startup* (Crown Business), Reis points out that the reason most startups fail is that they run out of money before they find a viable business model.

Now you may argue that you don't work for a startup. Maybe you work for a well-funded medium-sized company, or a Fortune 500 behemoth. These companies have more than enough resources for everything on your list, right? The thing is, though, even in these larger companies, your project is in constant competition with every other good idea the executive team has or hears about. So all projects are *always* at risk of cancellation or downsizing.

If your funding could be diverted to somebody else's bright idea at any moment, what do you do? You ruthlessly prioritize your work so that you get the most important things done first and begin to demonstrate value quickly. *Opportunity cost is when you never get the chance to do something important because you chose to work on something else instead.*

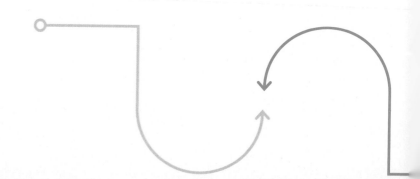

Shiny Object Syndrome

What about doing things in parallel? With sufficient resources, couldn't Brenda's company have done her little project alongside the move to support bigger customers?

We work with a lot of companies that are—like this company was—just coming out of the startup phase. They've been acquired, or gotten funding, or reached profitability and are looking to add to their product line or expand their market. A lot of them suffer from a lack of focus. Either they have 100 number-one priorities that the CEO somehow magically thinks they can pursue in parallel, or the priorities shift from day to day, or even hour to hour. What the startup CEO sees as responding with agility to opportunity, the development team secretly refers to as *shiny object syndrome*.

What the developers intuitively know is that there are a lot of hidden costs to any given development effort. Sure, you can build a feature that wins you a deal in a different segment from your target market, and you can probably figure out how to build it quickly on a shoestring. But then what?

Every feature you build has a carrying cost. For each new feature, you may have to:

- Retest (and fix if necessary) the feature with each new release and in each supported environment

- Document the feature

- Produce training material for the feature

- Handle support requests from customers (and train the support team to handle them)

- Figure out how to incorporate the feature into your pricing

- Figure out how to demo and sell the feature (and train the sales team)

- Figure out how to position and market the feature (and train the marketing and channels teams)

It's hard enough for an organization to do all of this well for a core feature set and a core target market. Imagine having to duplicate this effort for small numbers of customers in a variety of nonstrategic customer segments. The cost in distraction alone is huge, but never mind that. Adding all of this overhead means each individual effort slows down. The added overhead means that doing two things in parallel makes each take twice as long—and usually even longer due to communication, coordination, and mental switching costs.

Exponential Test Matrix Growth

Have you ever noticed that the more features your team develops, the longer it seems to take to develop the next one? Why is that? We've mentioned a lot of factors here, but the testing matrix is a large contributor. As you add features, you add the burden of testing not just each feature, but each feature in combination with every other feature. In software, this is commonly called *regression testing*, and unfortunately the size of this test matrix grows *exponentially* with the number of features (or modules or compatible third parties).

What does this mean? Think of it this way. If you have one feature, you have only that feature to test. If you have two features, you must test both individually, and also together (so now the number of tests is three). If you add a third feature, the number of test combinations rises to seven. So far, no big deal, but the numbers begin to rise rapidly from here, roughly doubling each time you add a feature. (For the math nerds, the progression is $2^n - 1$.) The test matrix for 5 features is already 31. For 10 features, it is 1,023. And to make your product go to 11 requires 2,047 test combinations. (Maybe that's why Nigel Tufnel's amplifiers don't go any higher.)

In practice, testing teams can't manually run through every possible combination every time, and so automation and sampling help reduce the amount of work involved, but in principle you can see how quickly the overhead of maintaining features and capabilities grows with every addition (Figure 7-1).

Brenda wasn't proposing a feature, but she *was* proposing having the company split its attention by marketing to, selling to, supporting, and possibly developing features demanded by a segment that had proven to have low ROI.

The inverse of (and antidote to) shiny object syndrome is focus. If you focus as an organization on one set of problems for a strategic set of target customers, you minimize the increasing drag of bad decisions and seemingly small diversions.

Have we convinced you that prioritization is critical to success? We hope so. The next step is how to prioritize—but let's start with how *not* to.

Features Versus Tests

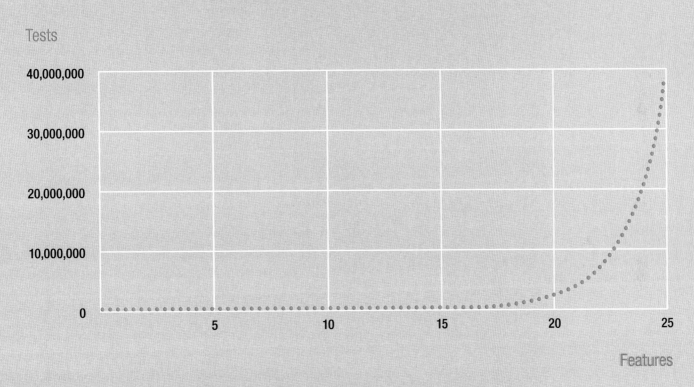

FIGURE 7-1. *The size of the test matrix grows exponentially with the number of features*

Bad (but Common) Ways to Prioritize

A good product person spends much of their time gathering data as input to good requirements and good priorities. They talk to customers, prospects, investors, partners, executives in all departments, salespeople, support reps, analysts. The list is never-ending, but the best decisions come when you have all the right inputs, and (as you'll see shortly) when you involve stakeholders in the process.

That is not to say that product management is a democracy or some kind of commune-like decision-by-consensus process. Not at all. In fact, letting others define your strategy is one of the most common mistakes we've seen in product planning. Other common pitfalls, or *anti-patterns*, include prioritizing based on the following factors

Your, or someone else's, gut

Prioritizing solely on your or some other executive's gut instinct can be a killer for team productivity and morale, and it usually results in high turnover, low productivity, and subpar results. Why? Two reasons. First, the lack of rigorous analysis means that the executive in question is very likely to change their mind, confidently proclaiming that X is the future, only to make an equally confident claim for Y a few days later. Second, while your CEO or other founding member of the executive team may have once been close to customers (or even been one at some point), their day-to-day experience is likely different now, and they are no longer in touch with the market.

A product person must learn to take executive gut opinion as input and apply some rigor to it, understanding what problem the executive is trying to solve, whether solving this problem aligns well with the product strategy, and whether the proposed solution is the best available. It is then often necessary to explain politely why, while this is not a bad idea, there are others that take higher priority.

Analyst opinions

You probably know more about your business and your customers than industry analysts do, and it seldom pays to substitute their judgment for your own. In the early 2000s, analysts projected that prices for flat-panel monitors would remain high for many years due to limitations in the supply chain. This was a logical but flawed straight-line extension of existing trends that failed to take into account the emergence of a few high-volume Chinese producers. Today, monitors can be had for less than $200 that only a few years ago sold for over $1,000. Take the time to do your own research and analysis, and you will be ahead of yesterday's trends.

Popularity

We truly believe that outsourcing your product strategy to your customers is a mistake in nearly all situations. An inexperienced product manager will, with the best of intentions, rank feature requests by frequency or size of customer. It makes sense, initially. Why not give customers what they ask for? The issue with that is customers can't often articulate what they need from your product. Yes, a seasoned product person will seek to understand customers and their needs—but this is fundamentally different from asking customers what they want.

Steve Jobs is famous for ignoring market research, saying, "A lot of times, people don't know what they want until you show it to them." This perhaps oversimplifies the problem a bit but resonates with our experience. A roadmap made up entirely of customer requests generally results in a product with no focus, unclear market positioning, and poor usability. If you understand what underlying problems motivated your endless list of customer requests, you and your team can usually develop a more elegant set of solutions that render that list moot.

Sales requests

As author and Silicon Valley Product Group founder Marty Cagan says, "Your job is not to prioritize and document feature requests. Your job is to deliver a product that is valuable, usable, and feasible." Similarly, asking for input from your sales team is smart—they have insight into how buyers think and what will get their attention—but prioritizing based on what will help close the deals in the pipeline this quarter is short-term thinking. It may help make the numbers once or twice, but successful product people are focused primarily on how to serve a market rather than individual customers.

Carol Meyers, CMO of Rapid7, says: "You can lock yourself into creating something that really only one company needs. Maybe nobody else really needs it. I think it's a big part of deciding who your real target customer set is and how that fits in with your business." On the other hand, everything is a spectrum, as Meyers points out: "Some companies only serve the biggest of the big, in which case, their roadmap often is totally determined by a couple of large customers because that's the focus of their business." Even then, we would argue, these companies depend on your expertise in devising the best solutions to their underlying problems. This dictates a two-way dialogue between a product producer and a product consumer. Otherwise, you are running nothing more than a custom development shop.

Support requests

The customer support team is a terrific source of insight for product people. Many can provide you with a list of common complaints or trouble spots in your product, ranked by frequency or rep time spent. This is good data for prioritizing enhancements under the general heading of usability, and it makes a lot of sense to prioritize work here if usability is one of your key goals. Take special note of that "if," though. We are not questioning the value of usability in general, but we are suggesting that this goal needs to be weighed in the context of *all* of your goals. A particular focus on usability makes all the sense in the world when you have a product people are buying but not using or not renewing sufficiently. It is probably not your #1 priority, however, if customers find it easy to use but it's missing critical functionality that causes them not to buy it in the first place. In that situation, feedback from current customers doesn't help you expand your appeal to prospects.

Competitive me-too features

The quickest way we've found to reduce the value of your product is to get into a tit-for-tat feature war with your competition. Once you and they are easily comparable, you have collaboratively created a commodity market where the guys with the longest feature list and the lowest price will win (though whoever makes it to the bottom of this race to the lowest price will have little to no profit margin left). Much better than trying to match the competition feature for feature is to differentiate yourself with capabilities perfectly matched to your chosen customer's needs and which your competitors can't or won't match. Thus, as the best (or ideally only) option for your particular niche, you can charge based on the value you provide rather than a few dollars less than your nonexistent competition.

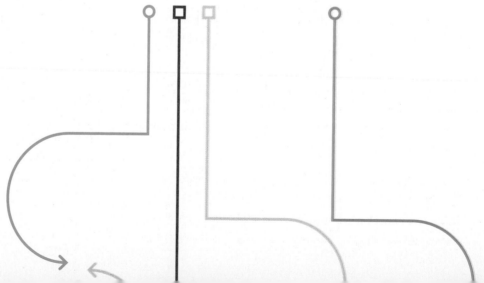

Prioritization Frameworks

Fortunately, there are also some *good* ways to set priorities, and some core underlying principles to prioritization that you can adapt to your needs. Here we've described a few that we've found useful, including critical path analysis; Kano; desirability, feasibility, viability; and (Bruce's favorite) the ROI scorecard. We'll also cover a related principle called MoSCoW, which helps you categorize your priorities once you've set them.

Throughout the discussion we'll describe when you might use each framework, but you should use your own judgment, test different approaches, and see what each teaches you about your own thinking—and then mix and match!

Critical Path

As we discussed in Chapter 3, a user journey map provides an opportunity for product professionals to tease out various dimensions at each step in the customer's journey, including their emotions and state of mind during each moment. Negative emotions can help you uncover key pain points and home in on those that are causing the most distress. These hot-button aggravations are often what brings users to the breaking point and convinces them to find a better way to do something.

Once you've identified those critical pain points, your job is to insert your elegant solution into your potential customer's path at the exact moment when their pain or frustration is highest. Like a marathon volunteer handing out water and energy bars at the bottom of a big hill, a product person needs to understand the major struggles in the customer's journey and offer the right solution at the right time.

Your goal is to answer the question, "What is the one thing (or set of things) our solution needs to get right?" These are the most painful steps in the process that you have to address or improve in order for the user to be convinced to hire your solution. You might identify numerous negative emotion states in your user's journey, but the key here is to narrow those down to the "must haves." Linking these key moments together into a *critical path journey* gives you a blueprint for creating a great product (or what some would call a *minimum viable product*).

Let's look at a real-life example.

In the middle of 2016 my team was approached by a new startup called BarnManager for help with strategy and design on a relaunch of their product (see Figure 7-2). The founder of BarnManager, Nicole Lakin, grew up riding horses and competing in hunter-jumper competitions. Lakin was in a unique position to empathize fully with her customers. After years of both owning horses and working in barns, she noticed a large majority of facilities still relied on whiteboards and notepads to communicate between staff, and traditional manila envelopes and filing cabinets to store records. Over time she realized these outdated tools were causing all sorts of problems for horse management teams.

First, due to the constant demands and frantic pace of horse management, many miscommunications would arise. For example, a discussion would happen between two people, but they would forget to inform the rest of the team. Or worse, a decision would be made but no accountability would be assigned and important tasks would go undone. These misalignments led to losses of time and money, not to mention undermining team chemistry and morale.

Second, managing paperwork had become a big issue. On any given day, a horse team could be inundated with vet visits, ferrier reports, competition forms, treatment plans, prescriptions, feed supplements, x-rays, ultrasounds, and much more. Without a consistent and reliable way to collect and share this information, horse teams again wasted time and money. Even worse, they lost critical information needed to properly care for a horse. In some cases, the mismanagement of these elements led to health issues for the horses that could have been avoided (or even untimely death in extreme cases). Other pain points for barn management teams included things like scheduling, hiring and retaining talent, travel logistics, and ordering supplies.

During the user research portion of this project, we worked to understand the journey of each key role, including owners, barn managers, groomers, vendors, and more. We attended competitions and helped shuck stalls. We spent hours poring over notes and folders, and shadowed team members as they went about their days.

We uncovered a lot of pain points and had many pages of notes, numerous sketches, and dozens of interview transcripts to prove it. There were a lot of valuable things we could have included in an initial product design, but when we finally had enough information to understand the full ecosystem, we were able to clearly identify the critical path pain points.

In this case, we realized that at a bare minimum BarnManager's new product had to provide a secure and easy-to-use repository for horse records. Through our research we were able to determine that if Lakin's team didn't get this right, the rest of the pain points didn't matter. Without a solution for digital record keeping, there was no way the low-tech horse management world would adopt a new software product. (We also realized that if we got this right, there was ample opportunity to improve on other important pain points down the road.) Once we identified our critical path was to solve for record keeping, we were off to the races (please excuse the cheesy pun)!

—Evan Ryan, 2017

Critical path for existing products

BarnManager was a brand new product, designed from scratch around the customer's critical path needs. However, this approach can also be helpful in prioritizing enhancements for an existing product or *growth product.*

We've seen too many talented product people make the mistake of forgetting that user behaviors, needs, and preferences change rapidly—*including in response to your product!* As a customer gets comfortable with your solution to the needs that initially prompted them to choose your product, new needs may become the critical path. Now that BarnManager solves the worst pains around document storage, perhaps their users feel the pain of daily communication more keenly. This may be an opportunity to expand the value of your application (or, if you ignore this, an opportunity for a competitor to use the new critical path to get in the door with your customer).

Staying in touch with your users helps you understand trends and anticipate new needs. There are many strategies for seeking direct customer feedback, from focus groups to surveys to product demos to A/B testing and more. As a product person, you will experiment and find the tools that work best for your team. Even in today's data-driven world, however, direct contact with the customer is as important as it was in Sam Walton's early days. That hasn't changed, and we encourage all product people to interact regularly, and face-to-face if possible, with actual human customers.

FIGURE 7-2. *BarnManager*

Kano

The Kano model, developed by Dr. Noriaki Kano, is a way of classifying customer expectations into three broad categories: expected needs, normal needs, and exciting needs. This hierarchy can be used to help with your prioritization efforts by clearly identifying the value of solutions to the needs in each of these buckets.

The customer's expected needs are roughly equivalent to the critical path. If those needs are not met, they become **dissatisfiers**, and your chosen customer will not buy your product. If you've met expected needs, however, customers will typically begin to articulate normal needs, or **satisfiers**—things they do not strictly need in your product but that will satisfy them. If normal needs are largely met, then exciting needs (*delighters* or *wows*) go beyond the customer's expectations. These typically define the offerings of category leaders. Table 7-1 shows an example of applying the Kano model to a common automobile feature.

One thing to bear in mind is that over time, expectations rise. There was a time when intermittent wipers were exciting (the 70s, anyone?), but now they are pretty, well, *normal*. In order to continue to differentiate themselves, high-end brands like Mercedes-Benz had to develop something even better, a rain sensor that adjusts wiping frequency automatically based on how much rain is falling on the windshield.

Needs	Example
Expected (Dissatisfier if missing)	Windshield wipers
Normal (Satisfier)	Intermittent wipers
Exciting (Delighter)	Rain-sensing wipers

TABLE 7-1. *How the Kano model might be applied to one automobile feature*

Figure 7-3 illustrates how customers' satisfaction and perception of product quality increases as the product moves from expected to normal to exciting needs. Note that in most cases, merely meeting expected needs is not sufficient to get out of the *dissatisfied* half of the diagram. This is especially true in a competitive market, where the customer can choose among several adequate solutions. Customers have high expectations!

The Kano model is most useful when you're trying to prioritize among customer needs based on the customer's own perception of value—for example, when you've covered the critical path needs and you're trying to decide among other ideas of increasing value. *Perception* is the key word here. If the customer lives in an arid climate, rain-sensing wipers may seem unimportant to them, and there will be no delight. Using the Kano model (or any other model incorporating customer value) requires you to know your customer well. See Chapters 5 and 6 for more on understanding and solving customer problems.

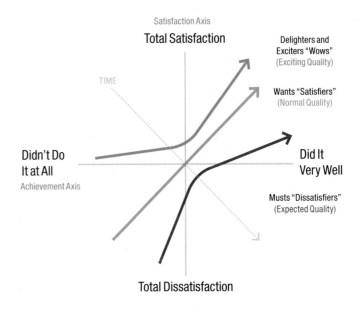

FIGURE 7-3. *Customers' satisfaction and perception of product quality increases as the product moves from expected to normal to exciting needs*

Desirability, Feasibility, Viability

While useful and popular, the critical path and Kano model by themselves are, in our view, insufficient to effectively judge the value of solving problems or of particular solutions to those problems. You must solve for critical path or expected needs (dissatisfiers) at a minimum, but that alone won't guarantee you success. Nor will you usually have the luxury to develop every satisfier or delighter you can think of. Resource and time constraints dictate that you pick among them and choose the ones that will make the biggest difference first.

One method we've used to prioritize potential solutions is to score each idea in terms of desirability, feasibility, and viability (see Figure 7-4).

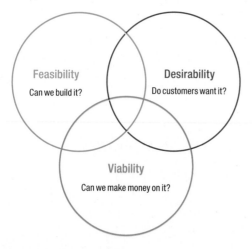

FIGURE 7-4. *Desirability, Feasibility, Viability Venn diagram. No product book is complete without this.*

Desirability

Desirability indicates the value to your customer of solving a problem, providing a feature, or performing a function. Things customers value most have higher desirability. (Counterintuitively, exciting needs have lower value than expected needs because the latter are absolute minimum requirements. The distinction between exciting needs and normal needs is trickier, and depends on the perception of value versus alternatives.)

Feasibility

Feasibility indicates how easy it will be for your organization to solve this problem, build this feature, or perform this function. Solutions that require more money, effort, or time to deliver have *lower* feasibility. (Easy stuff scores high.)

Viability

Viability indicates how valuable this solution is for your organization, often measured in revenue or profit. Solutions that make the company more successful have higher viability.

Using a simple 1 (low), 2 (medium), 3 (high) scale for each possibility allows you to add up the scores on each axis and come up with a composite score for priority. Ideas that score high on most or all of these criteria will rise to the top of the heap, above those that may score highly on one measure but not the others.

Let's consider an example. Imagine you are a car maker, and your proposed design already meets the minimum expectations for safety, performance, and economy. What should you add to make your cars more attractive to buyers? Table 7-2 shows how you might answer that question by calculating a potential feature's priority score based on desirability, feasibility, and viability. Perhaps customers have expressed a desire for custom colors and, based on your research, you give that a medium desirability score of 2 out of 3. However, manufacturing is telling you that they can't make colors to order without a separate paint process, which lowers both the feasibility (it's hard) and the viability (it will cost more and lower profits) to 1. The composite score is a disappointing 4 out of a possible 9.

On the other hand, your company has been investing in hybrid technology for some years, giving that a high viability score of 3. What's more, customers are clamoring for better fuel economy, driving the desirability up to 3 as well—and many are willing to pay a premium for hybrids, so profits are higher and viability is also a 3. This feature is a home run at a priority score of 9!

This method of ranking ideas may not be intuitive, but once you grasp it, it is simple enough to explain to your stakeholders (see Chapter 8) to gain alignment on which potential features or solutions meet all the core criteria for success—and which don't measure up.

Feature	Desirability	Feasibility	Viability	Priority Score
Hybrid drivetrain	3	3	3	9
Leather interior	2	2	2	6
Custom colors	2	1	1	4

TABLE 7-2. *Calculating an automobile feature's priority score based on its desirability, feasibility, and viability*

ROI Scorecard

The priority score was a perfect way to determine which of three potential car features to implement, but what if your feature list is dozens or hundreds of items long? Many product people are in this situation, and what's more, they often find that a lot of proposed features score an 8 or a 9. When you have too many good ideas, a simple prioritization spreadsheet known as an ROI scorecard can help you tease out and quantify finer differences in priority.

Fundamental to this approach is the concept of ROI, or return on investment. You can't do everything at once, so you should do the most leveraged things first—those that have the most bang for the least buck. This step can then provide funding for what you want to do next. We discuss how to define both *bang* and *buck* shortly, but the math is simple and intuitive:

Value/Effort = Priority

Value is the benefit the customer or the company gets out of a proposed feature or other change. **Effort** is what it takes for the organization to deliver that feature. If you get more benefit for less effort, that's an idea you should prioritize.

This is the traditional formula used in finance to justify dollar investments that have an expected future payout. If you think about it, that's exactly what we are doing when we invest time and money in employees to have them develop features or other product/service enhancements.

Consultants and product managers love a 2 × 2 grid, and it's easy to plot value versus effort this way and look for the items that fall deepest into the upper-right quadrant (see Figure 7-5). With a long list of features, though, this kind of chart can get pretty busy, so later we'll go over how the ROI scorecard can help you organize and rank ideas for improving your product.

Bruce has used models like this for years to set priorities based on relative ROI. He and others have used it successfully to prioritize features, projects, investments, lean experiments, acquisition candidates, OEM partners. He even used it once to figure out (and get his wife on board with) which car to buy. It seldom fails to support both the right decisions and (just as important) the right conversations. And at the right time, it helps frame up your business case. So next let's dive a little deeper into the equation underlying the ROI approach.

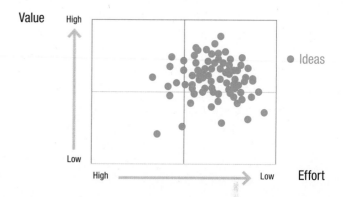

FIGURE 7-5. *Plotting Value versus Effort on a 2 × 2 grid*

Strategy defines value

The first part of the equation is value. In Chapters 5 and 6, we gave you guidance on identifying and solving for customer needs. Providing the critical path, satisfiers, and delighters that will attract and please customers is obviously a part of delivering value, but what's in it for you?

An equally important component of value is the benefit the company will receive from changing, adding, or enhancing some aspect of their product or service. As product people, we all assume that a better product will generate more success and more money for the company, but not all enhancements are equal in this regard. It makes sense to prioritize things that we expect to drive business results. This is similar to the viability concept we've discussed.

It's easy to be tempted into using dollars and cents here, and many companies judge the value of proposed work based simply on a revenue projection. But hang on—what if your product is pre-revenue and you need to focus on getting your core feature set in place? What if some of your customers are unprofitable? What if the mandate from your executive team is to grab market share? Or to enter a new and untested market? And even if revenue is priority #1, is new customer revenue or renewal revenue more important for your product? Revenue usually does come into it somewhere, but in most cases there are multiple drivers of value.

This is why we spent Chapter 4 talking about vision and objectives. If you understand customer's critical needs, and you've developed a set of business-outcome goals for your product, you have everything you need to define the value side of the ROI equation:

Value = Customer's Needs + Organization's Goals

Let's go back to our Wombat garden hose example from Chapter 2. You've determined that your customers have two critical path needs: reliable water delivery and reliable nutrient delivery. Delivering on either provides value, but delivering on both provides more value, and your team is busily working on features, materials, and manufacturing methods to meet these needs. If you could assign a simple score for each idea, rating how much you believe it will contribute to each goal, then you could add these components of value together simply.

You can do the same with your organization's goals. If your garden hose company has goals to grow new customer revenue and to increase the size of their addressable market, the expected contribution of proposed features can also be scored and added to the customer value scores, like this:

Value = CN1 + CN2 + OG1 + OG2

In this case, *CN1* is the first Customer Need, *CN2* is the second, *OG1* is the first Organizational Goal—you get the picture.

Deliberate imprecision

We can use a small range of numbers here, as we did when quantifying desirability, feasibility, and viability earlier. Once you get the idea of modeling decisions in math, it's easy to get caught up in perfecting your model. And since we are measuring business goals, which sometimes equate to money, it's tempting to try to be as precise as you can.

Be wary of complexity here, however. You are not actually trying to make a sales forecast or project schedule; you're merely trying to prioritize, so the need for precision is relatively low. You can always look more closely at the most promising ideas if you need additional validation before making a final decision.

In fact, much of the power of this model derives from this deliberate imprecision. Your team might argue about whether the revenue opportunity is $500K or $600K, but you'll usually be quick to agree on whether it is high, medium, or low. The math will work well with a 1–3 or 1–5 scale. However, 0 is also possible and quite useful when a particular idea seems promising for solving one problem but helps not at all on another. Bruce often employs a scale of 0 (low enough that it doesn't matter), 1 (medium or some positive effect), or 2 (large positive effect) to keep things as simple as possible.

A simple model is also easy for your stakeholders to understand. Try to make it so they can do the math in their head, so it's obvious when and why one thing scores higher than another. We've seen models with a dozen or more goals and types of effort, as well as complex weighting schemes that make using the model more difficult without adding much to its utility for decision-making.

The effort side of the equation

The second part of the ROI equation, *effort*, is whatever is necessary to meet your customer's needs and achieve your organization's goals by adding the proposed feature, enhancement, or solution. It is the reverse of feasibility, so in this formula, higher effort scores are bad.

Many product people who develop their own prioritization scorecard will leave out the effort side of the equation. Often they will say that business value is all that matters or that estimates are someone else's responsibility. We take issue with both of these claims. The reason is simple.

Let's say you have two proposals—two new feature ideas—that you estimate are about equal in adding value according to your scoring. Feature A will take three months of effort to deliver, but feature B will take only a couple of days. Isn't it obvious you should do feature B first, and start collecting that benefit while you are working on feature A? (Couldn't you actually use the money generated from feature B to fund your work on A?)

OK, you say, but I can't ask engineering for an estimate on every half-baked idea we might or might not ever do. They don't have the time for that and, besides, every time I ask for an estimate they want detailed requirements, and *I* don't have time for that.

Estimating effort without frightening engineers away

You're right, of course. Engineers are rightfully afraid of providing estimates for things they don't know enough about. If they've been around the block, they've probably been burned by a finger-in-the-air estimate (also known as a **WAG**, or **wild-ass guess**) that somehow turned into a commitment to a date when someone in management got hold of it.

A quick way to get over initial reluctance around estimates is to do the estimates yourself and then ask someone involved in the implementation for a reality check. By taking responsibility for the estimate, you absolve others from that feeling of premature commitment. (Also, it turns out it's much easier to get an engineer to tell you why you're wrong than to get them to give an estimate themselves.)

T-shirt sizing

One other thing you can do to get estimates without a lot of angst is to make them simple and abstract using *T-shirt sizing*. This common practice uses the familiar extra-small–small–medium–large–extra-large scale to roughly estimate the necessary effort without getting bogged down in sprints, days, or person-months—and if you assign numbers to the various sizes, it works well with the prioritization formula:

1 – Extra Small
2 – Small
3 – Medium
4 – Large
5 – Extra Large

Remember, you're not actually trying to schedule anything at this stage; you're just trying to prioritize. So a simple scale like this allows you to quickly gauge what things are promising enough to spend the time to get a real estimate on.

T-shirt sizing also borrows a principle from agile estimation using story points called *relative sizing*. It's not important whether a small is one to three weeks (or sprints or person-months). What's important for your prioritization formula is that it is small-*er* than a medium.

Think cross-functionally

In some cases, effort is simply the amount of time the engineering team will need to spend to code, test, and release the product. But usually there are other costs to consider as well. To get a realistic feel for the effort the company as a whole will incur, consider whether the marketing team will need to research and target a new market segment, or the sales team will need extensive retraining. Maybe you will need to strike a partnership with another company for a key component, or recruit new channel partners. The particulars will vary, but if you are trying to estimate ROI, you must think of the effort of the whole company. What good is a shiny new feature if your company can't market, sell, or service it?

Risks and unknowns

Just as you may run into a traffic jam or bad weather on a road trip, there are always unknowns in any product development effort. Especially in R&D efforts like software, you are building things that have never been built before, so there is no exact template, recipe, or blueprint to follow. Some teams build a fudge factor into their estimates to account for this. This risk factor applies (at least as well) on the value side of the equation because you cannot predict with 100% certainty how customers will react to your product before you've built it.

A risk factor can be used to discount the expected ROI of any proposed investment. A simple way to do this is to multiply the result of your value/effort equation by a *confidence* percentage. This is essentially the inverse of risk. You should be less confident about risky things.

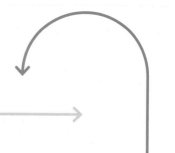

A Formula for Prioritization

The full formula for prioritizing investments in your product might look something like this:

$$((CN1 + CN2 + BO1 + BO2) / (E1 + E2)) \times C = P$$

| $\underbrace{\hphantom{}}_{\text{Value}}$ | $\underbrace{\hphantom{}}_{\text{Effort}}$ | Priority |

CN	=	Customer's Need
BO	=	Business Objectives
E	=	Effort
C	=	Confidence %
P	=	Priority

A simple scorecard

Let's put this all together now so that we can compare the ROI of proposed initiatives and derive a priority list. Scoring every job, theme, feature idea, initiative, or solution allows you to develop a scorecard ranking each against the others, as shown in Figure 7-6. (Just remember to compare only like things; it's hard to rank a theme versus a feature intended to fit within that or another theme.)

In this example, feature A ranks highly because it contributes to both goal 1 and goal 2 and has a high confidence. In contrast, feature B ranks lower despite the higher confidence because it supports only one of the goals.

Feature C has the lowest effort of the three and might have ranked higher, but it suffers both from low confidence and a negative score on goal 2. Why would a feature or other idea have a negative goal score? Sometimes, goals can conflict with each other. A given idea may contain an inherent trade-off such as quality versus quantity or power versus weight.

It is common, for example, in retail to discount prices to increase sales, but this comes at the expense of profit margin. Choosing to discount or not will depend on the balance of all your goals combined. In this example, another goal like unit sales or category sales may be the deciding factor.

$(CN + BO1 + BO2) / E = $ **Raw** $(CN + BO1 + BO2) / E \times C = $ **Score**

Feature	CN	BO1	BO2	E	Raw	C	Score
A	2	1	1	2	2	75%	1.5
B	1	1	0	2	1	90%	0.9
C	1	2	−1	1	2	40%	0.8

FIGURE 7-6. *A simple ROI scorecard*

A more complex scorecard

Now let's look at a ROI scorecard that's a little more detailed. Imagine you are in charge of a website called Plush Life that sells stuffed animals. You have a long list of ideas to expand your business, including enhancements to the site, expansion into China, and new concepts for toys to sell.

If you know your company goals are to increase sales, increase margins, and increase customer lifetime value (LTV), you can rank each idea against each of these three goals—and also against level of effort—to derive a priority score based on relative ROI.

The Plush Life scorecard is shown in Figure 7-7, you can build a similar scorecard yourself in Excel or Google Sheets.

Scorecard models can be built in a variety of ways. This one takes the basic concepts of desirability, feasibility, and viability, and rearranges them to create an ROI ratio between desirability + viability on the one hand and feasibility on the other. It also allows you to quantify separate components of each value (e.g., multiple aspects of desirability) and, finally, it adds confidence to account for risk.

Chapter 8 covers ways to use a scorecard like this to discuss and align on priorities with your key stakeholders.

So, to recap: when your proposed feature list is long, there are multiple factors to consider, and the answers are not obvious to everyone at first glance, the ROI scorecard approach can add just enough rigor to help illuminate and quantify subtler differences in priority.

IDEAS	GOALS (-2 to 2)			EFFORT (0 to 5)		Raw Score	PRIORITY (0 to 100) Confidence	Reqqs Score
	Sales	Margins	LTV	Dev	Merch			
Plushie of the month club	1	1	2	0	0	2	90%	180
Plush family sets	1	1	1	0	0	0.75	95%	71
Tweet adoptions	0	0	1	1	0	1	70%	70
Abandonment coupons	2	-1	0	0	0	1	70%	70
China drop ship location	1	2	0	3	0	1	65%	65
Cats vs. plushies video contest	2	0	1	0	0	1	60%	60
Accessories for plushies	1	0	1	0	3	0.67	90%	60
Panda Plushie	2	1	0	0	0	1	55%	55
Localized webstore	2	-1	2	2	0	0.75	70%	52
Ratings & reviews integration	1	0	1	3	0	0.67	75%	50
Referral points	1	-1	1	0	0	0.5	90%	45
Discount coupon support	2	-1	0	0	0	0.5	85%	43
Upload selfies	0	0	1	3	0	0.5	85%	43
						0.4	75%	30

FIGURE 7-7. *The Plush Life ROI scorecard*

MoSCoW

Whatever method you use in your prioritization process, you must communicate those priorities clearly to your development team. MoSCoW is a method for categorizing your prioritized list of requirements into unambiguous buckets, making it clear what your release criteria are. It has nothing to do with Red Square or St. Basil's Cathedral, but is an acronym for:

- *Must have*
- *Should have*
- *Could have*
- *Won't have*

Must-haves are requirements that must be met for the product to be launched. These are the critical path items or dissatisfiers—those expected needs without which no one will buy or use your product. These are also sometimes called **minimum-to-ship** features because (if you've classified things correctly) you can't launch until they are delivered.

Should-haves are not critical to launch, but are important and may be painful to leave out. Possibly including *satisfiers*, these are the last items you would cut in order to meet budget or deadline pressures.

Could-haves are features that are wanted, but not as important as should-haves. These are the first items you would cut if they introduced budget or deadline risk. You can distinguish could-haves from should-haves by the degree of pain that leaving them out would cause the customer, or the reduction in value of the solution. Another way some teams think of this category is as a list things to include "if easy." Your delighters may also fall into this bucket.

Won't-haves are requirements deemed "out of scope" for a particular release. Won't-haves could contain both satisfiers and delighters, but should not contain dissatisfiers or critical path items (otherwise, what's the point of releasing?). Won't-haves may be included in future releases, of course. It's useful to agree on these items up front to avoid misunderstandings about scope, rehashing scope mid-project, or what is often called **scope creep**.

MoSCoW is not itself a prioritization method, but we mention it here as a way to clearly communicate what your priorities mean in terms of release criteria.

Tools Versus Decisions

Numerical prioritization methods are controversial, and some experienced product people feel this left-brain approach can be misleading, providing a false sense of confidence in the math. Roger Cauvin, Director of Products, Cauvin, Inc., argues that this approach is an attempt "to address organizational dysfunction with formulas and analysis that ignore human factors" or to make up for a "lack of a shared understanding of the product strategy." He contends that a scorecard approach tends to "distract the team from a singular focus on delivering the product's unique value proposition."

We agree that many organizations claim to be data-driven when they are actually seeking data to support political decisions. In our experience, however, introducing the structure of a scorecard often forces a team to clarify, articulate, and align on their strategy and the value proposition so that they can effectively pick the right columns for the scorecard.

Some participants in roadmapping workshops have said "I can make these numbers look however I want." We have found that going through this exercise tends to reduce the amount of opinion and emotion in discussions of priority, forcing people to frame their arguments in terms of relative contribution to common goals. A scorecard approach makes it clear to everyone that there are multiple criteria for success and that the ideas that hit on all or most of them will be winners.

All of that said, no one should be a slave to a formula. Frameworks like these should be used as an aid to decision-making, not as the decision itself. Table 7-3 outlines some limitations to be aware of when using a scoring approach to product decisions.

TABLE 7-3. *Scoring pros and cons*

Cons	Pros
Scoring lots of little features or requests could provide a false sense of confidence or progress.	Scoring items being considered anyway forces discussion of the underlying problems and the value of solving them.
Simple scale misses finer differences.	Simplicity keeps teams from arguing over unimportant details.
Keeping to a few goals misses important factors that should be considered.	Forcing teams to narrow down to a few goals forces them to face the reality that they can't do it all.
Scoring models do not include intangible factors such as generating "buzz" or level of "innovation."	Objective criteria supports a more rational and open discussion of trade-offs.
Scoring models do not include dependencies, resource availability, or promises made to key customers, the board, Wall Street, and so on.	Scoring models uncover where resources and promises do not align with priorities.

Dependencies, Resources, and Promises (Oh, My!)

If you've done a good job selecting and leveraging one of these frameworks, your resulting priorities should be directionally correct, but they will require an additional layer of practical considerations before they can be scheduled for work.

You may be forced, for example, to begin with an item that your model says is your #2 or #3 priority, for reasons that have nothing to do with dissatisfier, must-haves, or ROI. It may be that certain critical resources required for priority #1 will not be available until a future date, or that #1 is dependent on #2 being completed. It may also be that priority #47 has already been promised to the board of directors or written into a customer contract.

These additional factors don't affect priorities, per se, but they can affect scheduling. It's simple to make notes on such details in the margin of your scorecard, and then refer to them when sitting down to plan out the sequencing in the roadmap.

Prioritization Frameworks

TABLE 7-4. *Priorization Frameworks overview*

Framework	Use To	Choose When	Downsides
Critical Path	Identify the "one thing" that will drive a customer to buy	Designing an MVP or making a major expansion in product scope	Does not take into account effort, risk, or business goals; does not rank needs finer than "critical" or "noncritical"
Kano Model	Understand how customers perceive relative value	Identifying possible add-ons or enhancements	Does not take into account effort, risk, or business goals
Desirability, Feasibility, Viability	Identify opportunities that meet all key criteria for success	Prioritizing among a relatively small set of initiatives or solutions to a particular problem	Categories are not clearly defined in terms of customer needs, organization goals, or different types of effort or risk
ROI Scorecard	Rank ideas according to return-on-investment criteria	Weighing multiple factors and/or a long list of possible initiatives, problems to solve, features, or solutions	More complex model requires alignment on different components of value and effort
MoSCoW	Communicate launch criteria	Feeling uncertain about what must be included in a product, service, or release	Does not help set priorities, only communicate them

Value/Effort = Priority

Summary

Companies that consistently prioritize and focus on a few highly leveraged initiatives invariably learn faster, grow larger, and become successful by getting everyone pulling in the same direction. You can't do it all, so pick your bets thoughtfully.

Don't fall into the trap of prioritizing by gut feel or outsourcing your decisions to your customers, competition, or industry analysts. Use one of the frameworks described here to develop, get input on, and make decisions about priorities in an objective and transparent way. Table 7-4 provides a quick summary of what each approach is best at and when you might choose to use it.

Regardless of which prioritization framework you use, how you order items on the roadmap will reflect your priorities, and make them starkly clear to your customers and other stakeholders. It's important that you can explain why you've chosen these items and placed them in this order, so use these frameworks wisely and, as we describe in Chapter 4, keep your timeframes as loose as you can to preserve your flexibility.

With all of this information in place, you are ready to begin laying out a roadmap that will drive you quickly and efficiently toward your goals and your vision of a successful product—that is, one that adds value to customers' lives and businesses.

First, however, you're going to need buy-in. In the next chapter, we will discuss how to use both shuttle diplomacy and group workshops like design sprints to drive organizational alignment and gain the buy-in you'll need for your roadmap to succeed. We'll also show you how to leverage your prioritization framework to facilitate that cross-functional work.

Chapter 8

Achieving Alignment and Buy-in

What you'll learn in this chapter

What alignment, consensus, and collaboration mean

How shuttle diplomacy can help you obtain input and buy-in

How to use a roadmap co-creation workshop to achieve alignment

How to use software applications to align teams

Chapter 8

Achieving Alignment and Buy-in

"No plan survives contact with the enemy," said Helmuth von Moltke the Elder. We would add: "or your stakeholders."

You can create the best plan ever conceived, but it will work only if the people who fund it, execute it, and receive its output believe in it.

I was a product manager at a biotech startup years ago, and we were developing a new product that enabled our customers to extract and work with viral RNA. There was a software component that had to be written, optimized, and tested, as well as a reagent recipe that had to be refined and tested, all before release.

We were a 75-person company in total, so thankfully it was a relatively small team. However, separate teams were developing the software and reagent pieces, and the sales team was constantly begging me for release dates and sometimes directly reaching out to software or R&D. They had sales targets to hit and customers who were asking for the product. I had four other products in development, all utilizing the same finite software, research, and testing teams. My solution for all this? I created an Excel spread-sheet and listed out the products, product features, and release dates, then sent it by attachment to my colleagues.

Problem solved. I was a genius!

Not so fast.

I caused quite a few fire alarms with the sales team and the software engineering team. Surprisingly, the research team developing the reagents was actually thankful. I was curious: why was one team fine with my Excel spreadsheet while the others seemed enraged? Maybe the research team just wanted spreadsheets? Why were sales and engineering so upset?

—C. Todd Lombardo, 2006

What C. Todd created with this spreadsheet was not a product roadmap, but rather something more akin to a release schedule. Schedules are great. As humans, we love predictability: the train arrives at 3:04 p.m.; my flight leaves Monday at 5:14 p.m.; the meeting is at 10:30 a.m. Having something to refer to is important, but if that artifact doesn't match up to others' expectations, get ready for some heated conversations.

Lacking any other knowledge of product strategy (hey, it was early in his career!), C. Todd thought his schedule seemed the most rational approach, as it was intended to bring certainty to stakeholders who were clamoring for it. We all want permanence in an impermanent world. *Silos*, which is what C. Todd created when he went off on his own to make that Excel file, can kill enthusiasm and momentum for many things, especially a product. Unless you're a company of one, you need your team to be on board with you. There is no substitute for a roadmap (and by now you know this differs from a release plan/schedule, or we haven't done our job very well), and in order to create a roadmap, you need buy-in and alignment.

During the buy-in process, you'll polish off the prioritization exercise you began in Chapter 7 and then prepare to document and share the roadmap to a broader range of stakeholders. The fact that the entire team has the opportunity to offer input will lower friction as you move toward alignment.

There's no one right way to achieve buy-in, but there are definitely wrong ways to go about it. For example, although it might sound tempting to your caveman brain, beating everyone over the head with a stick works about as great as using molasses to brush your teeth. We won't get into tall negotiation strategies and interpersonal tactics here. There are many other well-researched and well-written books for that. The three main vehicles we've seen successfully used to obtain alignment and buy-in on product roadmaps are shuttle diplomacy, meetings and workshops, and software applications (or some combination thereof).

Before we get into those approaches, though, we need to define exactly what we mean by *alignment*.

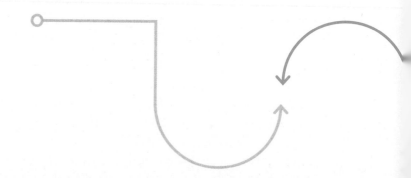

Alignment, Consensus, and Collaboration Walk into a Bar…

When we talk about alignment, we often think consensus or collaboration. They are similar yet different terms.

Alignment

This is a concerted effort to help people understand the issues and what their respective roles are. It means asking questions and listening to feedback both from the internal product team as well as external stakeholders. People with differing opinions can still align on their intentions. Alignment is not consensus.

Consensus

In theory, this means a group of people reaching a mutually agreed-upon decision. In practice, it often means hours of discussion leading to decisions that everyone *supposedly* agrees to, but that no individual can be held accountable for ("I didn't vote for that!"). Once the decision has been made, if someone doesn't like it, they can often be a barrier to its implementation.

Collaboration

This is when individuals cooperate to accomplish a common goal or outcome. Individuals work together for a shared purpose—they may not concur on everything each step of the way, but they do agree on the final outcome.

What do you need when you are a product person looking to get a roadmap in place or updated? Alignment and collaboration. You don't need consensus to get your roadmap in place. Let's repeat that: *you do not need consensus to get your roadmap in place, nor do you need it to update your roadmap.*

Let's continue with more detail on your stakeholders. We discussed in Chapter 3 the importance of identifying your internal (and external) stakeholders, and it might be wise to map them out:

Now we're ready to get into the "how" of achieving that alignment.

Shuttle Diplomacy

Greg [product manager] had been there for two years before me when I took over product. He had been struggling with that team for ages, because they could never come to a consensus on anything.

Timing was on my side: the executives had just been to a board meeting and presented their goals for the next year to the investors where they had four very crisp business-outcome goals clarified. Two were product oriented—the two essential ingredients to differentiation of our product. The other two were business objectives.

For one, the CEO had said, "I want disruption. I want game changing." And the way I ended up translating that was "future potential revenue," as we knew for sure we weren't going to get revenue this year, but it was worth investing in because we might realize that [higher revenue] in the future. I was then able to do my prioritization matrix and sort everything in terms of things that looked like they had a high ROI to low ROI.

I went to each of the executives individually, and initially when I asked the executives about the goals they agreed, "Yes. Those are the goals." We actually managed to skip past the usually difficult phase of just agreeing on the goals. The prior meeting set up the goals conversation for success.

During each of those meetings, I got out my spreadsheet—my scorecard with the goals at the top and all the ideas—and made sure all their ideas were on the spreadsheet. We discussed each and scored the ones that they cared about. I made sure that they felt like they were heard and had a chance to contribute.

Finally, we sat the whole group down in the room, and we came up with a roadmap in about an hour and a half. Greg came out of that room, astonished, "How did you do that? That was magic. I've never gotten those guys to agree on anything." I replied, "It wasn't magic. It was shuttle diplomacy."

—Bruce McCarthy, 2011

Bruce's story is straight from the playbook of Henry Kissinger when he "shuttled" between Middle East capitals as he sought to ease negotiations in the fallout of the October 1973 war.

Kissinger leveraged international toll lines, the White House's hotline to Moscow, telegrams, couriers, recorded messages, transatlantic flights, and any other means of communication he could get his hands on. Because the parties could not—or more likely would not—speak with each other, Kissinger spoke to each of them individually. This turned out to be a blessing in disguise, as Kissinger could cut through any emotionally charged interactions and talk about things with them sympathetically and pragmatically. By acting as an intermediary and peace broker between the two sides, he appeared neutral and worked to incrementally improve the situation, rather than attempt a full-blown resolution.

There's a lot of debate about the long-term outcomes of the situation; however, the tactic proved very useful in highlighting stakeholder needs in the negotiation process. For years after the ceasefire, Kissinger continued shuttling between the major players, and his efforts culminated in the 1979 Camp David Accords, considered the first peace treaty between Israel and an Arab state.

Shuttle Diplomacy for Product People

Shuttle diplomacy involves meeting with each party individually to reach decisions that require compromise and trade-offs. This approach can help manage and coordinate stakeholders to reach agreement on what the current and future product will be.

Political negotiators employ shuttle diplomacy when one or more of the parties refuse to recognize another party involved in the decision. For product professionals, this won't likely be the case, although we've all had our share of teams where the friction is high. As a product person, you may find that (unlike some heads of state) your stakeholders are willing to meet together. However, we've found it's often better if they don't—at least at first.

Have you ever been in an executive meeting where each attendee is there just there to prove how smart they are? Or have you experienced it when the stronger voices in the room end up belittling or intimidating others? These political machinations can ruin your attempts at alignment. We've found the politics are much more manageable in one-on-one settings. Like Kissinger, you can focus the conversation on common goals if it's just you and them, with nobody else in the room for them to answer to or try to impress.

Why Does Shuttle Diplomacy Work?

At each meeting, identifying the individual's goals, priorities, and other considerations is the key to managing by shuttle diplomacy. These one-on-one meetings offer a feedback loop not only about the person's thinking, but also whether it is in line with the organization's goals and vision (see Chapter 4 on guiding principles). You build trust and rapport with each of these stakeholders, because you're listening to them and asking them why and how things are important to them. If they keep pushing for something that doesn't make sense in terms of the larger goals, that's a hint that there's an unwritten goal that needs to be discussed.

In addition, if there are any politics (or hidden agendas), an individual stakeholder is likely to reveal them to you if you're receptive and able to build a close rapport, whereas they might not in a larger group meeting. You take all of the office politics out of it, because it's just you and them talking about what's best for the company, and not them trying to sound smart in front of the CEO, team, or board.

Finally, by giving each stakeholder the opportunity to have input early on (i.e., while the product roadmap is still a work in progress), the shuttle diplomacy process gives them authorship of the plan too. It's not your plan anymore—it's *our* plan. The co-creative nature of the roadmap process cannot be understated.

How to Engage in Shuttle Diplomacy

As we've mentioned, when engaging in shuttle diplomacy, you should entice your stakeholders with a draft of your roadmap and ask for their input. In the first part of your meeting, always tie it to the goals and objectives. You can use the simple acronym GROW to guide your conversation:

Goals
What are they trying to accomplish in the next X months?

Reality
What's on their plate now? What's recent?

Options
What do they think will help them achieve those goals? What options have you already discussed that need to be revisited?

Way forward
Which of the options helps them achieve the goals they described earlier in the conversation? Which options are at the top of their list and why?

Shuttle Diplomacy Canvas

If GROW helps guide your conversation, the shuttle diplomacy canvas in Table 8-1 can help you track the meetings and move you toward final alignment and buy-in for your roadmap.

Here's how it works:

For each stakeholder, track their desired outcomes, why they have those objectives, what metrics they use in achieving those outcomes, and what their top product priorities are. Also be sure to make a note of any additional considerations, such as office politics. This canvas is not intended for you to share across your team; rather, it is a useful guide for you to track your one-on-one conversations.

TABLE 8-1. *Shuttle diplomacy canvas*

	Stakeholder		
	Joan, CEO	Mark, Sales	Jen, Engineering
Goals: What are their desired outcomes (objectives) for next 3 months? Why do they have those objectives? What metrics are they using to achieve those outcomes?	15% y/y growth in profit She's accountable to shareholders % Revenue increase and EBITDA	Hit $24MM in revenue in Q1 2017 Revenue keeps the company in business Revenue, average deal size	Grow team to meet new capacity, improve sprint velocity Need to optimize team productivity
Reality: What's currently on their plate?	Setting up company for scale	Missed last quarter's target and scrambling to make up	Three teams each with differing velocity, demands for multiple feature delivery faster
Options: What do they think needs to be on the roadmap?	Platform stability New features sales requested Better onboarding experience	Client ABC, Inc requested new features and possibility of closing a deal	Platform stability Bug fixes Sales feature request
Way forward: Which of their product priorities for the next 3 months are they in agreement with?	Platform stability Better onboarding experience	Better onboarding	Platform stability

What's Difficult About Shuttle Diplomacy?

So what's the downside to shuttle diplomacy? Simply put: the time it takes. Many consider meetings the bane of their existence and to add yet another one-on-one meeting may elicit an allergic response. The answer is to keep the meetings short and informal. Focus only on the issues a particular stakeholder cares about in the meeting with them, and ignore the rest of your list. Sometimes, a bunch of small meetings is actually easier to schedule than a big one with a lot of busy executives, but not always. Consider your organization and use your judgment.

Other potential challenges of shuttle diplomacy meetings include rapport and location.

Rapport

Some people you will get along with better than others. This is normal and natural. Your mileage may vary.

Location

One-to-one meetings are always better when you're in person than when you're remote. Sure, we all love (and/or hate) Google Hangouts, Go-to-Meeting, Join.me, Skype, WebEx, and Zoom, but there's no substitute for an in-person meeting, as you'll better build rapport with each stakeholder.

Even when you've met with each stakeholder one-on-one, you still may need to hold a meeting that brings everyone together. In fact, we recommend that you do this on a regular basis, perhaps every quarter or every year depending on the velocity of change in your business. This brings us to the co-creation workshop.

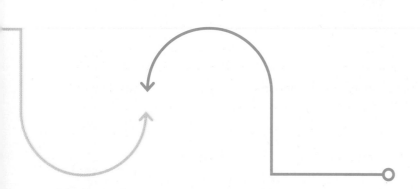

Meetings and Workshops

Once a shuttle-diplomacy process has been completed, pulling everyone together for a cross-functional meeting or workshop can be a very effective way to obtain final buy-in across the group of stakeholders. Likely there are some conflicts and trade-offs that will be made. This is normal and expected.

These meetings can be of two flavors: a formal presentation of recommendations or a co-creative workshop. Both serve to bring a team of stakeholders into alignment. This approach works with two key aspects: 1) when a culture exists that encourages constructive disagreement, so that people are comfortable voicing their opinions and leaders appreciate hearing them and 2) there is general agreement on the organization's overall strategy, so that stakeholders can agree on how to make decisions.

Presenting Recommendations

Emily Tyson, Vice President of Product at NaviHealth brings together a product portfolio review group to evaluate the business on a quarterly basis and ensure alignment with the business priorities. During this meeting, the team would examine recent progress, reflect that with proposed changes, and consider how to allocate or reallocate resources.

Prior to the meeting, each team then did a few things (they might sound familiar!):

1. Gathered their inputs from their stakeholders (a la shuttle diplomacy-like) with information such as: What are priorities for sales? What are priorities from the clinical team? What does security need in the roadmap?

2. Performed a T-shirt sizing exercise for each proposed initiative to gauge the level of resources needed to execute.

3. Assembled business cases to answer the following questions: What's the story around these initiatives? How does it fit with our company's vision, with the long-term strategy, with the near-term strategy? How do we think about the competitive landscape, or the development times the market? What are the factors we should be considering when evaluating these?

With that in place, the team would present their proposal to the portfolio advisory meeting with their recommendations. This approach, with lots of "homework" up front and a formal "this is what we're doing" to get sign-off from a steering committee or senior managers or executives is one way we often saw in larger, established organizations with a hierarchical structure.

Co-creation Workshop

Another approach we saw was to bring the stakeholders together for a workshop that is less of a present-the-plan and more a let's-figure-this-out.

A co-creation workshop can follow a shuttle diplomacy effort; it's a good way to bring all the stakeholders together to finalize the prioritization process. At times you may also be able to skip the one-on-one meetings and go straight to the big meeting/workshop—for example, teams where there are not a lot of stakeholders and/or where political agendas may not be overly prevalent might be well served by going straight to the workshop.

The workshop needs to have a clear plan and outcomes before you hold it. No one wants to go to another unnecessary meeting. Your outcomes are to finalize the roadmap for the upcoming period (year, quarter, etc.). You likely won't be doing this weekly, biweekly, or even monthly. Most teams we spoke with do this quarterly, especially in the software world, where it often takes about three months to create and release anything of substance (beyond bug fixes and minor feature enhancements).

Workshop agenda

A co-creation workshop might loosely follow this agenda:

Intro and rules—5 min

Hopes and fears—10 min

Vision and goals—10 min

Back-plan—15 min

Sizing and prioritizing—40 min

Wrap-up—10 min

The intro and wrap-up are self-explanatory, but let's take a closer look at the steps in between.

Hopes and fears

Hopes and fears is a simple exercise where each individual writes their hopes for the product's future on one color of Post-it note or index card and then writes their fears on another color (one hope/fear per Post-it or card). The objective here is to draw out everyone's emotional aspirations and fears and see how they align with each other and with the established business objectives. When we run this exercise, many types of visions (hopes) and roadblocks (fears) surface that otherwise would remain hidden or unsaid. Sometimes you just need to give people a platform to open up!

Vision and goals

If it is not already determined, an exercise to articulate the product vision could prove beneficial. As we discussed in Chapter 4, to articulate product vision, you can have everyone in the room follow this MadLibs prompt:

A world where the [target customer] no longer suffers from the [identified problem] because of [product differentiator] they [benefit].

And pare this down to:

To [benefit realized] by [product differentiator]

After writing this out on a large Post-it or index card, participants can then compare their responses. Or, as another option for establishing vision—taken from the book *Gamestorming* by Dave Gray, Sunni Brown, and James Macanufo (O'Reilly)—you can have participants complete the Cover Story exercise. Each participant draws the cover of a print or digital newspaper or magazine (e.g., *Fast Company*, *TechCrunch*, *Mashable*) five years in the future, after the roadmap has been implemented. What impact has this product made on the customer base? What change has it brought about? Make sure they include a headline, an image, a subheadline, a few sidebars, and a quote.

Back-plan

A great exercise to follow Cover Story or some other future envisioning exercise, a Back-plan starts with the end result of the cover story (i.e., the future that will result from the roadmap) and then works gradually backward to the present. Each step backward must be realistic, so teams are forced to think through all the different changes necessary. For example, if the product vision is that solo business travelers have a satisfying time dining with strangers while traveling, what's the first step backward from that? One option is that they have a way to search for a desirable local restaurant while traveling to an unknown area.

Sizing and prioritizing

Next on the agenda is a sizing and prioritizing step. One exercise that's helpful for narrowing down ideas is the $100 (or €, £, ¥, ฿, etc.) test, also from *Gamestorming*. In this exercise, each participant is given a limited amount of currency to "invest" in particular customer needs. A variation on this is to break down the aspects of each theme into desirability, feasibility, and viability, and then have only those responsible for each area invest in that category (so stakeholders invest according to their category). Then you tally up the results, as shown in Table 8-2.

For reasons we describe in Chapter 7, we don't believe voting is a good way to prioritize. It is, however, a good way to narrow your focus to a manageable list for discussion.

These are a mere handful of workshop exercises that can help bring a team into alignment. There are many others that can do similar, and these can help a team arrive at the final decisions together. Rather than having one person be "the decider" and enforce others to follow her or his decision, this co-creative effect helps to keep the team on-board because like shuttle diplomacy, each stakeholder had input into the final decisions.

	Desirability (Marketing, Sales, UX)	Feasibility (Engineering, Development)	Viability (Product managers)	Total
Theme A	$50	$25	$20	$95
Theme B	$25	$75	$60	$160
Theme C	$25	$0	$20	$45

TABLE 8-2. *Prioritizing by desirability, feasibility, and viability with the $100 test*

Software Applications

While co-creation workshops and shuttle diplomacy are the most common ways of achieving alignment, a number of teams use various software applications to help them do so. With distributed teams becoming more and more common, remote teams may not be able to engage in the classic face-to-face shuttle diplomacy or in-person co-creation workshops. While videoconferencing has improved remote communication, additional software products can go even further toward aligning teams. Some are specific product roadmapping tools, such as ProdPad, Roadmunk, Aha!, and ProductPlan, while others are communication and tracking tools such as JIRA, Slack, Google Docs, Asana, and Trello, among others.

"One of the significant areas we wanted to address was to ensure the work we were doing aligned with our larger goals and strategies. Our company used JIRA as our project tracking tool. It is a highly configurable system, so we were able to manipulate it to monitor our work across teams. While configurability can be a value, it can also be a curse so it was important to keep it as simple as possible.

We created a ticket type which contained the high level requirements of the problem statement to capture the details of our objectives. We also created a new scrum board in Jira which allowed us prioritize our objectives in quarter based sprints to connect our strategy roadmap with the work for the engineering team.

Each ticket was a dynamic version of a problem statement so as we continued to identify key learnings we were able to evolve our problem statement effectively around a what we were trying to measure, the measure of success, the impact of what we were doing and our expected return.

One key factor was a representative cross functional team that met weekly to bring in the perspectives of our Agile coaches, engineering leads, product managers, UX, and PMO team to ensure alignment, efficiency, and clarity.

In general, this approach gave us a dynamic view into what was being defined and delivered. I think that was a really important aspect of this cross-functional team. Roadmaps come in a variety of shapes and sizes, and separately each product manager had their own independent roadmaps. We needed a way to bring them all together in a single place where we could better understand the priorities to achieve our end-of-year goals, our longer term goals, and how we need to break that down into what we were doing right now to get there."

—Vanessa Ferranto, former Product Manager at Zipcar

By meeting weekly, the cross-functional Zipcar team raises issues, agrees on topics, and prioritizes/reprioritizes as necessary. They use JIRA to make inputs and track their progress. Thanks to this combination of recurring meetings and software applications, the team is able to tag, track, manage, and ultimately align on the product themes. This weekly meeting makes minor course corrections to a larger meeting that occurs quarterly, where decisions that have greater consequences may occur.

We spoke to several other teams and heard similar stories. Sameena Velshi, a product manager at Roadmunk, uses the company's own product to help with this: "To no one's surprise, we use Roadmunk. There's a feature that allows you to roll up multiple roadmaps into one. This allows us to separate out what is specific to our department from the more company-wide vision."

Velshi's team receives updates through the platform and determines how to change course as needed, and the software helps teams to comment and approve or change the priorities on their roadmap. No team we spoke with relied solely on a software product for obtaining alignment, but the communication of information across a platform aided the buy-in process.

Summary

In this chapter, we covered some important concepts around alignment and buy-in. First, we clarified some definitions—namely, you learned that *alignment*, *collaboration*, and *consensus* are not the same thing. It's crucial that you understand the differences between these terms and are aware of the downsides to consensus.

Next, we discussed three mechanisms to achieve alignment: shuttle diplomacy, co-creation workshops, and software applications.

Shuttle diplomacy involves meeting one-on-one with each stakeholder.

Co-creation workshops, by contrast, bring everyone together in a structured, intense session focused on alignment. Teams with a smaller group of stakeholders or fewer political agendas can choose to skip the one-on-ones of shuttle diplomacy in favor of moving right to the co-creation workshop.

Finally, software applications such as JIRA, Roadmunk, ProdPad, AHA, and ProductPlan can help with digitally tracking and obtaining buy-in from stakeholders. Most often, however, some form of face-to-face meetings is necessary for teams to achieve alignment. One tip: don't reconsider the decisions made unless there is significant new information. This keeps the teams working to activate and execute on the decisions agreed upon.

At the end of the day (or should we say, beginning of the quarter), no matter which of these approaches you use—shuttle diplomacy, co-creation workshops, and/or software applications—you'll need to get your team and/or organization aligned on the direction your product is going. Once you've done that, you're ready to formalize, publish, and distribute your roadmap. Chapter 9 will cover tips and techniques for sharing your roadmap within your organization, presenting it to stakeholders, and revising it to incorporate the feedback you receive.

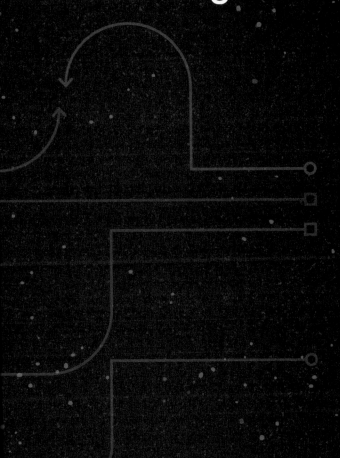

Chapter 9

Presenting and Sharing Your Roadmap

What you'll learn in this chapter

Why to share internally

Why to share externally

Risks of sharing

Whether to develop multiple roadmaps

How to present your roadmap to stakeholders

Chapter

9

Presenting and Sharing Your Roadmap

Every stakeholder will benefit from a view into what's coming, and an opportunity to contribute

One of the chief functions of a product roadmap is to get everyone excited about the future. To accomplish that, you have to tell the story.

By now you know a product roadmap is not a release plan, nor a backlog, nor a list of features. The components we've presented give you all the raw materials in place to develop a good roadmap

If you have been following this book chapter by chapter, you now have all the raw materials in place to develop a good roadmap. This chapter will walk you through the process of sharing and presenting it. Once you've shared the first cut of your roadmap, as with most iterative processes you will probably need to revisit and revise parts of it, so we'll also cover what to expect from that step.

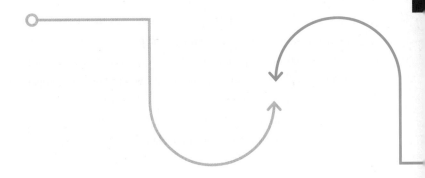

Why to Share Your Roadmap Internally

Of course, you're thinking, *at a minimum I have to show my roadmap to my boss, my boss's boss, and whatever team will be doing the work*—and you're right! However, as we discuss in Chapters 3 and 8, there are many other people in your organization, outside this core group, who will benefit from seeing your roadmap.

Every department—from sales to marketing, from support to finance, from manufacturing to operations, from engineering to business development—will benefit from a view into what's coming, and an opportunity to contribute. We outlined the needs and expectations of each group in Chapter 2, but now let's discuss the advantages of sharing the product roadmap broadly within the organization.

Inspiration

One of the chief functions of a product roadmap (and one of the key skills of a successful product person) is to get everyone excited about the future. Remember that product vision concept we discussed back in Chapter 4? There's a reason for it: your roadmap will paint a picture of a world where your customers are happy and your company is successful, making everyone in the organization want to be a part of it. If your *why* (aka product vision) is compelling, and your *how* plausible, you've got people hooked, and they'll be happy to discuss how they can add their particular *what* to the plan.

Alignment

In product-driven organizations, the roadmap forms, or at least informs, the planning of activities all across the organization. It tells marketing what they can announce at the next industry conference. It tells sales when they'll have something new in their bag. It tells customer support when training will need updating. It tells manufacturing when they'll need new tooling. You get the idea.

Even if the feedback loop goes in the other direction, and other functions are driving timing and priorities, the roadmap presents an opportunity to align across these functional boundaries as well. Getting everyone pulling in the same direction and with the same timing is like coordinating the rowers on a crew team: it's critical to moving forward swiftly.

The IKEA Effect

As we discussed in Chapter 8, presenting the roadmap early and often to stakeholders around the organization is critical to getting feedback and buy-in. Whether you use a co-creation workshop approach, shuttle diplomacy, or a combination of techniques, involving people from across the organization in the development and refinement of the product roadmap will radically increase buy-in. Why do people love their IKEA furniture? Because they had a hand in putting it together. It's the same with roadmaps.

Why to Share Your Roadmap Externally

If your customers were as inspired by your vision of the future as you and your team are and if they aligned their plans for buying, adopting, and using your products with your plans for delivering them that would be amazing, right?

Jeff Bussgang, General Partner at Flybridge Capital, recounts his experience as a product person at a company called Open Market, which went public in 1996.

"We were a leader in the early days of internet commerce. The product was originally built using the TCL scripting language—quite useful for prototyping and quick implementations.

We went public and skyrocketed from zero to close to a hundred million dollars of revenue. The growth was great, except the code base was absolutely falling apart and not scaling because of the scripting language we used. Customers became really unhappy and our engineers couldn't add features fast enough to keep up with the competition. We had a billion dollar market capitalization and a total house of cards for a technical foundation.

We decided to do a flat-out re-architecture. When you do a rewrite, you're basically running in place. You're not adding features; you're just re-implementing things in a more scalable, extensible fashion.

Our product roadmap really helped us because we articulated that the rearchitecture would not just better for us internally, but would also be better for our customers. The software architects authored an internal document that described how we we would do the rewrite and deliver exactly the same functionality. I had to reframe that document to be customer centric and articulate to customers how the rewrite would add a lot of value to their business, not just address our internal problems."

The rewrite took Open Market a year to complete, so they were asking for a lot of patience from their customers in a very competitive market. Jeff clearly understood his customers' needs, however, and was able to sell them on his product vision.

"It was all about extensibility. Re-writing it in C++ would allow for APIs that you could then extend into new, important areas. You could integrate better with your existing systems. The original version of the product was a very closed system and as e-commerce became more central to all of the business operations, we were able to articulate the value in the roadmap to get customers to work with us and sell through this difficult period."

Though Bussgang's was an extreme case, in enterprise software, the team that is implementing your solution for the customer really needs some understanding of what's coming and when, so they can prepare their organization for the upcoming changes.

They can also become advocates for you, paving the way and smoothing over internal politics and purchasing roadblocks for any future releases.

The Risks of Sharing

Overpromising and Underdelivering

A lot of folks worry that anything they share on a roadmap will come back to bite them later—fearing that, as Drift CEO David Cancel, puts it, "I'm going to disappoint you by giving you exactly what we thought six months ahead of time was the best solution when it's not, or by changing course and having lied to you."

But Janna Bastow, CEO of ProdPad, argues that "as long as we're open and honest about our priorities, customers are actually very forgiving. We hold onto the feedback we get and reach back into it to guide the way we approach their problems—and our customers know that. Roadmap conversations have helped us understand what resonates with people, and that helps us position our launches down the line."

"The reason the product team has a roadmap is partly because it's a sales tool, a communication tool to help customers understand what's coming so that they can plan for it. We actually could not land contracts without some level of comfort developed in the customer around that.

"What we put on the roadmap is: we're going to have an initial version of this thing ready to use. That did a couple of things. For us, it prevented us from needing to build the whole thing up front and figure out the entirety of it. For them, it let them look at a timeline and say, April 1st they're gonna have something we can look at. And it prevented either of us from having to agree that this thing will solve all future problems.

"So what's the purpose of the roadmap then?" she asks. "For us it was to allow the customer internally to align around the idea that we'd given them the date, without actually tying the delivery of something to that date."

This is very similar to the idea of themes, presented in Chapter 5. You want to communicate your direction and intent clearly without committing to deliverables that may not be achievable or may not even be the right solution to the problem in question.

The Osborne Effect

Announcing future plans too early can also slow down current sales as people may decide to wait for the next version or upgrade. This is more prevalent with hard goods that can't upgraded with a simple software update, increasing the perception that the current product will soon be obsolete. This phenomenon became known as the Osborne Effect after sales of the Osborne 1 computer fell sharply in 1983. Founder Adam Osborne had pre-announced new models that would outperform the existing model and dealers canceled existing orders for the first model in anticipation. The new models did not appear quickly enough and the company soon declared bankruptcy.

Competition

And what about the competition, you ask? Isn't it risky to tell the market what's coming? Sure, there may be good reasons not to put everything on your roadmap, especially if some of those themes can indicate a product direction that may further differentiate you, but if you're simply making existing product areas more robust, it may be OK or even necessary.

For example, imagine you are a component manufacturer for the mobile device industry. You sell specialized chips for phones, tablets, watches, and the like. Your customers—the makers of these devices—plan their products out many months or even years in advance, including the performance specs, price points, and unit volumes. If you want to win their business, you have to be open about those kinds of details with them on their timeframe. To quote Sasha Dass, Technical Program Manager at Analog Devices, "In our business, you better not show up to a customer meeting without a detailed roadmap."

This example has less to do with the pace of change in the electronics industry (which is accelerating all the time), and more to do with the commitment a customer is making to your product and to your company when they buy. The electronic device makers in question here need to be able to count on your company to deliver on your roadmap over time, or they risk missing their own launch dates and sales forecasts. Millions of dollars are at stake, and they want to know you will be there for them.

Samuel Clemens, VP of Product Management for InsightSquared, says, "The roadmap is never ever allowed outside the building. However staff can use the roadmap to respond to a customer that, 'yes, something is on our short-term roadmap; or: our PMs are looking for more input on that so would you mind doing a call with one of them?'"

If you want your sales team to focus on selling what's in the warehouse right now, but you also want to position things properly for changes you know are coming, Bill Allen, former Product Manager for Bose, has some sage advice. If someone asks about, for example, support for an emerging standard, tell them, "It's a great thing. It's fantastic. You've all heard it, you'll all love it. But let's really look at the reality of this. Right now, the ability to use this feature is a rare occurrence. The chances of you actually being able to enjoy it are maybe 5%. Do you really want to say that that's a must have feature just yet?" You may still choose not to discuss future products, but you've established that you'll be ready when and if this new standard becomes important, while removing the customer's fear of buying something without it now.

So there are advantages and risks in sharing a roadmap externally. Given that, how do you decide what, if anything, you should share? Janna Bastow created a neat chart that illustrates, by role, how much detail and which initiatives you should share (see Figure 9-1). In general, the further away from your core product development team you get, the less detail about features, functions, and dates you should provide, and the less you probably want to share about brand-new product directions and internal infrastructure work. (Refer back to Jeff Bussgang's story at the beginning of the preceding section, though, for an exception!)

Who should see your roadmap?

FIGURE 9-1. *Janna Bastow's chart showing how much detail and which initiatives you should share, by role*

Multiple Roadmaps? Not So Fast!

As we've outlined, most organizations have multiple stakeholders who would benefit from a view into your direction and strategy. The trouble is, each has different things it cares about most.

So do you need to prepare a different roadmap to present to each group? And if you did, wouldn't that defeat your efforts to align the organization around a common cause? The answer is to build the specifics each group wants to see *on top of the common foundation* of your vision, strategy, and themes.

If your roadmap is expressed in a slide presentation (as many are), this might mean the first four slides apply to all audiences, but there is one additional slide dedicated to each group. This is where the complementary information that provides additional context and detail to the roadmap itself comes in. Keeping these separate but including them in the same document makes a clear and direct link from the overarching story to the details a particular stakeholder group cares most about.

With this modular approach, it's not a question of whether to share your roadmap, but of which portions you show to whom.

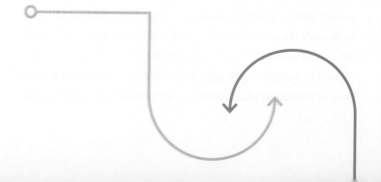

Presenting the Roadmap to Stakeholders

OK, you've shared your vision, your strategy, and some vague ideas about themes, timing, and so on. Terrific. But then come the questions. What features are you actually going to ship? What are the release dates?

What can the sales team demo at the next big trade show? What are the revenue projections? The dependencies? Risks? The channel strategy?

You've piqued your audience's interest, and now they are hungry for details. Can you answer them? Should you? The level of detail you give in the answers to these questions depends on who is asking and your confidence in your information.

It also depends on a good collaborative back-and-forth between you as the responsible product person and each stakeholder. We outlined the primary components of the roadmap in Chapter 2 and described the secondary components as optional. Next, we describe which stakeholders care most about what optional data and how much detail to provide. We also outline a third group of complementary information that, while not formally part of a product roadmap, can provide important context to your discussions with these stakeholders. We'll discuss ways to incorporate or at least acknowledge the information that will help drive alignment across your organization and with customers and partners.

Sharing outside your core team may sound risky. We've found, though, that as you get into these discussions, your roadmap will change for the better. It will mesh symbiotically with stakeholder needs, leverage serendipitous events, generate new ideas, and most important, drive alignment by getting all the groups on the same page (literally, if you print out your roadmap!).

What the Development Team Needs in a Roadmap

In a software company, your development team consists of the engineers, designers, testers, and operations people who will actually build and deploy your product. (We would generally include your technical support team in this bucket as well with regard to information needs.) In a hard-goods organization, the design and manufacturing teams perform a similar function. These sorts of folks need concrete information on which to base project schedules, resource plans, technical architectures, and supply chains.

Your high-level thematic roadmap is great context for them, but it is not enough by itself. These teams want something that begins with your high-level story but then embellishes it with details including likely features, stage of development, scalability expectations, dependencies and risks, and even information about the technical underpinnings of the work they will be executing on (see Figure 9-2).

Bill Allen, former product manager at Bose says, "Engineering cares about your product roadmap because, oh we're moving into Bluetooth? We'd better do some research into Bluetooth. Oh speakerphone? We know about microphones, and we know about speakers, but we don't really know about speakerphone or how to integrate them together in a speakerphone. There's going to be a new disc formats? Is it going to be Blu-ray or is it going to be HD DVD? How do we decide? When do we need to make that choice? Technology roadmaps and decisions are always informed by the product roadmap."

(Facing page) A roadmap can include technical information, but should start with the timelines and themes of the general roadmap. It then adds the details the development team needs to do their planning, including likely features, stage of development, scalability concerns (such as anticipated usage), dependencies and other risks, as well as technical and infrastructure work needed to support the themes.

Product Roadmap for Engineering

● **Features & Solutions**
Though not yet certain, the features that will support the themes through 2018 are being actively explored within the development team and are shown here for discussion.

● **Stage of Development**
Pre-production on the Indestructible Hose has begun, so few changes are possible before launch. Later themes are in earlier stages and are likely to evolve.

● **Product Areas**
Each product area may have its own team or parallel development path. Calling them out facilitates planning and coordination among teams. There is only one Wombat team, however, so we have left them out of this roadmap.

● **Scalability**
Knowing the expected sales volumes allows the team to plan production capacity in advance, directly influencing the size and timing of additional plants.

● **Technology & Infrastructure**
When and where we need to build plants to support volumes, as well as when materials and other technologies need to be ready to support themes.

● **Dependencies and Risks**
Anything that could interfere with the planned roadmap items goes here.

FIGURE 9-2. *Product Roadmap for Engineering*

THE WOMBATTER Hose

PRODUCT VISION
Perfecting American lawns and landscapes by perfecting water delivery

H1'17	H2'17	2018	Future
Indestructible Hose ● Features: • 20' & 40' lengths • No-leak connections • No-kink armor ● Stage: Pre-Production ● Technology & Infrastructure: Santa Fe contract plant	**Delicate Flower Management** ● Features: • Super flexibility • EZPlace stakes • Low-pressure mode ● Stage: Prototype ● Technology & Infrastructure: New Mesa Plant	**Putting Green Evenness for Lawns** ● Features: • Microfine dispersal sprinkler • Dispersion pattern management • Rain sensor ● Stage: Discovery ● Technology & Infrastructure: Cincinnati plant online	**Infinite Extensibility** Technology & Infrastructure: Pressurization technology
	Severe Weather Handling ● Features: • Antifreeze interior • Frost-proof skin • Hardened connectors ● Stage: Materials Testing Technology & Infrastructure: Severe weather skin	**Extended Reach** ● Features: • 100' length • 2-way grip connectors ● Stage: Discovery	**Fertilizer Delivery**
● Volume: 100k units	● Volume: 1m units	● Volume: 4m units	● Volume: 10m units
● Dependencies & Risks: Clare sick for 3 weeks	● Dependencies & Risks: Untested materials	● Dependencies & Risks: 2nd plant required	

Update 3/20/17, COMPANY CONFIDENTIAL, not for distribution

Secondary Components

Features and solutions

Though we avoided committing to specific features for most audiences in Chapter 6, the development team needs some idea of what they will be building in order to plan their work. A short list of features you believe will effectively address the market problems laid out in your themes will add the necessary level of concreteness to your roadmap, while allowing the development team to ballpark the effort involved and negotiate with you over scope and timing.

When you first show this roadmap to your team, you are looking for their feedback about what is feasible, not dictating what must be complete by certain deadlines. For example, you may have seven ideas for features that you believe will help with your "time savings" theme. However, the team may come back after scoping each and tell you that there is room for only the first four in the next quarter. You can then have a productive discussion about whether to hold the release until the following quarter to get all seven, have two releases, or ship those four and move on to another theme.

Stage of development

As we discussed in Chapter 6, the stage of development your product is in dictates certain things about your priorities, so being clear about the product's stage in your roadmap sets helpful context and expectations for the development team.

In the earliest stages, the product is under active development and may not have any users outside the company while the basic capabilities are being laid down. Later, the roadmap may be changing rapidly as early customers provide feedback on unmet needs. Custom features for large customers may become necessary in the growth stage, and the later stages may focus entirely on compatibility updates and bug fixes.

Armed with information on what stage you expect the product to be in at various points in time, your development, operations, and/or manufacturing teams can plan resource allocations accordingly.

Product areas

In addition to ensuring coverage across the key parts of the product as described in Chapter 6, development teams often use product areas as an organizing principle for their internal teams. One team may focus on the administration UI, for example, while another focuses on search, and a third on transactions.

Including this information on your roadmap in the form of tags, colors, or swim lanes makes it easy for your development team to map your roadmap to their organization, facilitating collaboration.

Complementary Information: Platform Considerations

Scalability

Engineering, operations, and manufacturing teams need a good understanding of the volumes you expect and when you expect them. This is obvious in manufacturing, where plant capacity can be a gating factor to growth. In software, however, the ability to accommodate a certain volume of users—known as *scalability*—is often overlooked by product people.

Think about it this way. A prototype of your product can probably be produced very quickly. It will look great and perform well as long as there are only a few users on the system at a time. On the other hand, a system can theoretically be designed to support almost any number of users, but it will take proportionately longer to design and develop. If you are specific about how much usage you expect at what stage of the product's life, you and your development team can find the right balance between those two extremes for each stage, reducing the risk of failure without overengineering the solution.

Technology and infrastructure

As the product grows in popularity, it also usually becomes more complex with the added features and functionality demanded by its expanding customer base. This puts strain on the underlying technical infrastructure as it is asked to support features and functions for which it was not originally designed.

Imagine you buy a starter house with one floor, one bathroom, and no garage. Over time, as your family grows, you begin adding rooms, but eventually your lot is full, and you can no longer expand outward. You need to add a second floor, but you discover that your foundation wasn't designed to handle the additional weight. You need to make some changes below ground before you can expand upward.

In manufacturing, changes in volume, design, or materials may require retooling at the plant. In software, this situation is sometimes referred to as *technical debt*, and may require rewriting or refactoring parts of the code. And if the problem is more extensive, it may require a rearchitecture or replatforming before more features or more users can be added effectively.

This sort of work is hidden entirely from the customer but may sometimes require a large percentage of the resources available for roadmap work. It's best to work with your internal team to identify this technical and infrastructure work and build it into your plans along with the more visible work it supports. Some teams create a separate row on the roadmap for this supporting work, assigning them their own themes or concrete deliverables, while others create a separate slide or document for it.

Complementary Information: Project Information

As we stated in Chapter 1, a roadmap is not a project plan. When you're working with the team in charge of the actual project, though, it can pay to surface key project elements such as schedule, resources, dependencies, risks, and even status. We recommend working with a partner from your development team (a project manager, team lead, engineering manager or someone with similar responsibilities) to develop and present this information briefly after you've set the stage with the primary and selected secondary components.

Schedule and resources

The lines, arrows, and connectors of a Gantt chart do not form a good roadmap. Nor do the burndowns, burnups, and velocity trackers of an agile release plan. Your development team may use these or other tools, however, to manage and communicate about the projects that will eventually allow you to deliver on your roadmap. Working back and forth together between the roadmap and the project or release plan will allow you to check your assumptions and be more realistic about dates while challenging the team to deliver the most value.

Dependencies and risks

If an item cannot be solved for or built until something else is solved for or built, you must factor it into your sequencing. For example, imagine you're building an application that helps youth athletes keep track of their progress in a sport. One theme on your roadmap might be "Record practice performance" and another one might be "Measure performance over time." A user would not be able to see a report on their performance over time without first having recorded their performance for each individual training session, so the sequence is dictated by this dependency.

In addition, dependencies among teams are the most common sources of delay in project schedules. It's therefore important to identify those that could affect your ability to deliver on your roadmap as early as possible so they can be prioritized, and so contingency plans can be developed.

Other sorts of risks include resources that may be in short supply, unproven technologies or materials, untested suppliers, unpredictable usage patterns, even unproven assumptions about the market.

The example roadmap slide in Figure 9-2 has a single row for this, but many roadmaps include an entire slide on risks and mitigation plans.

Status

On-track or behind schedule; green, yellow, or red: these sorts of status updates on the projects related to your roadmap should be the subject of frequent discussion with your development team. They are not part of the product roadmap, but as it becomes clear over time what solutions will be delivered when, they do inform it. Dates may shift or the list of six features for the next important theme may become four. Depending on how detailed you've been about dates and features, these changes may or may not need to be reflected on the roadmap—but you as the product person must understand their implications.

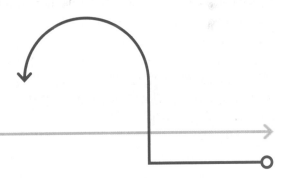

What Sales and Marketing Need in a Roadmap

Whereas your development team wants hard details about what they have to build, your sales and marketing teams have their own sorts of planning to do—usually around generating revenue. After you've set the stage at a high level, your roadmap should help them understand what advantages your product will provide in terms of increased value, tied to critical dates on their calendar (see Figure 9-3).

Secondary Components

Stage of development

Just as the development team benefits from understanding the stages of your product's development, so too do the sales and marketing teams. This principle was brought home to Bruce McCarthy very strongly when a sales VP he worked with surprised him by asking to delay the launch of a new product.

Bruce had assumed that the revenue opportunity presented by the new product would provide a welcome boost to the VP's efforts to make his numbers as the end of the year drew close. This VP had the experience to know, however, that an untried product, no matter how well conceived, was bound to go through some rough patches as the sales pitch, pricing, packaging, and materials were refined. He also knew that a new product re-

quired an investment in training for his people, which meant time away from closing deals.

In the critical year-end period, this savvy manager wanted to maximize the output of his team by focusing their time on selling proven products with an established sales methodology. He was happy to launch a new product in the first quarter when the pressure was off and the team would be going through annual training anyway.

Leading up to that January launch, Bruce was able to convince his sales VP to let him work with one sales specialist on an early access, or *beta,* program for the new product. Marketing and sales teams usually care about a product when they can begin talking about it, and with a beta program this actually comes before a full launch.

Even a rough idea of the timing of these milestones will allow your sales and marketing teams to plan promotion and sales training calendars with your product in mind. Later stages of the product's life may inform sales quotas and campaigns designed to open up new markets.

Many products take months or years to generate significant traction because the sales and marketing teams are not prepared to generate or convert demand when the product first becomes available. Collaborating with these teams on launching activities plans starts with the roadmap.

Product Roadmap for Sales & Marketing

- **Features**

  The features for the Indestructible Hose are 90% locked down now and Marketing and Sales can begin discussing how to promote and sell them. Features for later themes are much less certain and are not ready to discuss outside the development team.

- **Target Customers**

  Knowing where and to whom your product will be sold is critical information for your sales and marketing team to plan effectively.

- **Confidence**

  Want to prevent Sales from over-promising? Make sure you communicate your level of confidence in the items on the roadmap.

- **External Drivers**

  These opportunities for promotion and demonstration are fixed in time. Showing them here provides context for discussing what will be ready when.

THE WOMBATTER Hose

PRODUCT VISION
Perfecting American lawns and landscapes by perfecting water delivery

H1'17	H2'17	2018	Future
Indestructible Hose **Features:** • 20' & 40' lengths • No-leak connections • No-kink armor **Objectives:** • Increase unit sales • Decrease number of returns • Decrease overall defects **Stage:** Pre-Production	**Delicate Flower Management** **Objectives:** • Double ASP **Stage:** Prototype	**Putting Green Evenness for Lawns** **Stage:** Discovery	**Infinite Extensibility**
	Severe Weather Handling **Objectives:** • NE Expansion **Stage:** Materials Testing	**Extended Reach** **Stage:** Discovery	**Fertilizer Delivery**
Target Customers: Santa Fe & Phoenix	**Target Customers:** Southwest and Northeast regions	**Target Customers:** US & Canada	**Target Customers:** Pro market
Confidence: 90%	**Confidence:** 75%	**Confidence:** 50%	**Confidence:** 25%
External Events: Partner Showcase Apr 19	**External Events:** Lawn & Garden Show Jun 15	**External Events:** Hardware Show Jun 23	

Update 3/20/17, COMPANY CONFIDENTIAL, not for distribution

FIGURE 9-3. *The roadmap you share with your sales and marketing teams starts with the same timelines and themes as all views of the roadmap, then adds details of interest to them, including stage of life, success metrics, how particular steps in the roadmap affect them, and external events that coincide with releases*

Target customers

As your product's capabilities grow, you may be able to expand into new markets and serve new types of customers. In fact, once you have a product out the door (as we explain in Chapter 4), expanding your addressable market is one of your most effective growth levers.

The roadmap you share (and codevelop) with your marketing and sales teams should describe when the problems you're solving will allow you to effectively serve new customers. "Prosumer features" or "Localized for China" are the sorts of things your internal go-to-market partners will view as opportunities, and you will want to give them time to prepare to take maximum advantage

Confidence

Salespeople are speaking directly with customers every day, and they are eager to please. You can easily imagine how something on the roadmap could work its way into a sales conversation, so it's important to provide context about how firm the information is. As described in Chapter 6, you can easily manage these expectations (and keep casual conversations from becoming promises) by adding a confidence percentage to the items (or timeframes) on your roadmap, indicating how likely they are to be delivered in that timeframe (or at all).

Marketing teams planning for the next quarter's campaigns will also benefit from an indication of how certain you are about what's coming in that timeframe. They'll know not to book an expensive spokesperson for a special event built around something on your roadmap until your confidence is above 80%.

Features and solutions?

Your marketing and sales teams may have good intelligence on what it will take to meet these market segment or competitive positioning needs. So it makes sense to involve them early and give them at least a little visibility into what features you have in mind to fulfill those needs. Just be careful about how specific you are. Although these teams are internal to your organization, it is their job to speak to customers, and you don't want them to get ahead of your certainty. Use words like *likely*, *probable*, and *tentative*, and make liberal use of your confidence percentages.

Complementary Information: External Drivers

While you want to reserve as much flexibility as you can for your development schedule, there are many types of external events over which you have little or no control. Regulatory changes may drive compliance requirements, industry events may be opportunities for new product announcements, user conferences may require demos of forthcoming enhancements, and competitor announcements may drive changes to your priorities.

Mapping these sorts of events out as well as you can in advance can help ensure the best timing for items on your roadmap. Again, they are not part of the roadmap itself, but including them as supplemental information can help the marketing and sales teams prepare for these events. (They can also help you prioritize roadmap items.)

What Executives Need in a Roadmap

Executives and members of the organization's board of directors are generally concerned with the investments the company is making and the expected return on those investments. Their interest in and tolerance of the more operational details of all of this are inversely proportional to their trust in the team's ability to execute. In other words, if they are digging into the details, it's because they think something is wrong.

Generally, then, you want to limit the roadmap information you provide to these stakeholders to the high-level initial material on vision, strategy, and problem-solving themes. It is smart, of course, to have all of the details on hand for those occasions when an inquisitive board member develops some concerns. Even better, you can anticipate those concerns by previewing your high-level material with these stakeholders and asking for feedback or questions in advance. (This is another use of shuttle diplomacy, discussed in Chapter 8.)

Complementary Information: Financial Information

Market opportunity

Some of the most compelling internal roadmaps describe how each step along the journey brings them closer to success in capturing their market, driving up their revenues, and generating profits.

This might take the form of a target customer, as in the sales and marketing version of the roadmap, or it might include explicit revenue and profit targets. (See the Contactually roadmap in Figure 9-4 for an example of an objectives-driven roadmap.)

Profit and loss

Some product people act more like general managers for their particular product, carrying profit and loss responsibilities they must report on regularly. Even where this is not the case, executives and board members often want to understand the general magnitude and timing of anticipated revenues that will pay back the investment they've made in a particular product development effort.

Business plan pro formas are not part of a roadmap, but adding rough revenues and a projected break-even timeframe can be useful to help this audience understand what you feel is required to reach a certain level of financial results.

Product Roadmap for Executives

- **Market Opportunity**
  Expanding the market for your product expands the size of your opportunity, something your executives and board of directors will be pleased to see.

- **Profit and Loss**
  The timing and magnitude of expected financial results can provide meaningful context to the roadmap for the folks who fund it.

THE WOMBATTER Hose

PRODUCT VISION
Perfecting American lawns and landscapes by perfecting water delivery

H1'17	H2'17	2018	Future
Indestructible Hose Objectives: • Increase unit sales • Decrease number of returns • Decrease overall defects Stage: Pre-Production	**Delicate Flower Management** Objectives: • Double ASP	**Putting Green Evenness for Lawns** Stage: Discovery	**Infinite Extensibility**
	Severe Weather Handling Objectives: • NE Expansion	**Extended Reach** Stage: Discovery	**Fertilizer Delivery**
Market: Santa Fe & Phoenix	**Market:** Southwest and Northeast regions	**Market:** US & Canada	**Market:** Pro market
Opportunity: $200 million	**Opportunity:** $2 billion	**Opportunity:** $4 billion	**Opportunity:** $7 billion
Revenue/Gross Profit: $5 million/[$7.5 million]	**Revenue/Gross Profit:** $50 million/[$2 million]	**Revenue/Gross Profit:** $200 million/$15 million	**Revenue/Gross Profit:** $200 million/$15 million

Update 3/20/17, COMPANY CONFIDENTIAL, not for distribution

FIGURE 9-4. *A roadmap for your executives or your board will help you make the case for investment in your product by showing how your planned enhancements will expand your market opportunity*

What Customers Need in a Roadmap

We've discussed the pros and cons of sharing, including disappointments, competitive concerns, and Osborning, but it's worth a final note here on what customers really need from you in a roadmap. They might *ask* for details about features and dates, but in most cases that's not what they really *need*.

Bruce enjoys recounting the story of a dashing Spanish customer who challenged him to reveal whether a particular feature would be included a particular release. One of the themes on Bruce's roadmap at the time suggested that possibility but, in full fencing stance, this reseller demanded a commitment in front of a group of other customers from around the world. He didn't quite throw a glove on the floor, but things did go a little quiet in the room as Bruce considered his answer.

"I understand why that feature is important to you and to your users," he said, projecting his voice a little for the crowd. [This was true. He'd had conversations with many such end users.] And it's one of the things we're looking into as a way to allow you to [solve a particular problem] as I mentioned in my roadmap presentation. However," he went on as more and more people halted their conversations to listen in, "we want to solve the problem in the best way possible for everyone, and I don't want to limit the team's options by specifying a particular approach too early."

This got a general murmur of approval, but it did not completely satisfy Bruce's challenger. "When will you commit?" he demanded after a beat. Fortunately, Bruce knew they could be pretty confident about the content of a particular release a quarter ahead of time, so he was able to provide a general answer along the lines of "most likely by the end of the year." As others went back to what they'd been doing, he spoke to the man individually and offered to help manage expectations with his executives and users.

Customers and prospects can be this demanding, and much more at times. Many prospects will refuse to sign—and longtime customers will refuse to renew—if certain features are not committed to. How you handle this depends on your business, but we encourage you to ask what your stakeholders are really wanting you to commit to. Is it really a particular feature or a specific date? Or is that they want to know you have skin in the game, too? Or that you are listening to them? Or that you'll give them more information when you have it? Offer to help them with their real need as Bruce did here, and maybe they'll give you some slack on the roadmap.

And remember that the more commitments to specific deliverables you make on the roadmap, the less flexibility you have to adjust course when the winds change—and lack of flexibility is not in your customer's interest either.

Product Roadmap for Customers

- **Timeframes**

  We've removed the "Future" column and its themes altogether here because they are entirely devoted to the professional market and this roadmap is for consumers. It's important to focus your message on what's important to your audience. Instead, we've included a column about the improvements made in the past, to remind customers of our track record of delivering value.

- **Features**

  Since the features for the Indestructible Hose are fairly certain, showing them to customers is a low-risk way to get feedback on how they are perceived. It may be too late to change them in production, but it's not too late to change how they are positioned and sold.

THE WOMBATTER Hose

PRODUCT VISION
Perfecting American lawns and landscapes by perfecting water delivery

2016	H1'17	H2'17	2018
Flexi-Hose Enhancements	Indestructible Hose	Delicate Flower Management	Putting Green Evenness for Lawns
Features: • 3 inch-radius turns without binding • Eco-safe polymers • 5 new colors	**Features:** • 20' & 40' lengths • No-leak connections • No-kink armor	Severe Weather Handling	Extended Reach

Update 3/20/17, subject to change without notice.

FIGURE 9-5. *The roadmap you share with customer will be greatly simplified. It should not include the details internal stakeholders need but instead focus exclusively on the value these customers should anticipate you will deliver to them in the future. And if you have more than one type of customer, you will want to divide up the roadmap along those lines, showing only what's relevant to the group you are presenting to at the moment.*

The Roadmap Presentation

You've done your homework, and now it's time to present your roadmap. If you've developed your guiding principles, uncovered and solved for customer needs, and prioritized your ideas, you probably have something pretty great at this point, but now it's showtime.

How do you ensure a good reception for your ideas?

Preparation.

Here's a short roadmap presentation prep checklist:

1. Identify your audience: Peers? Executives? Have they seen the roadmap before? If so, what input have they had?

2. Clarify your goals for the presentation: What do you need from this meeting? Are you looking for input on an early draft? Alignment on a particular aspect? Or just informing people of what's coming?

3. Determine what your audience cares about: What level of detail is necessary? Do you need to summarize the roadmap details to only the high level? Are you presenting a portfolio of products?

4. Assemble your components: Pull your product vision, business objectives, themes, and timeframes all together. Consider which secondary and complementary components are necessary based on your audience (#1) and what they care about (#3).

For your presentation, the following sequence might be useful:

1. Start the presentation with the *why*, and be sure everyone is on board with the product vision before you move on to details. Cover recent progress—what's been completed since last time? Don't forget to include emotion! Use quotes or anecdotes from customers on how the changes to the product positively impacted them.

2. Show what's in the near term and clarify what critical needs justified the prioritization and aligned with the business objectives. Add stories of sales, support, and customer requests to help humanize the product and give meaning to why you're doing this—beyond making some chart continue to move up and to the right (emotion + data + stories = win).

3. Propose what's in store for a longer term and continue to reinforce how this will align with the company's objectives.

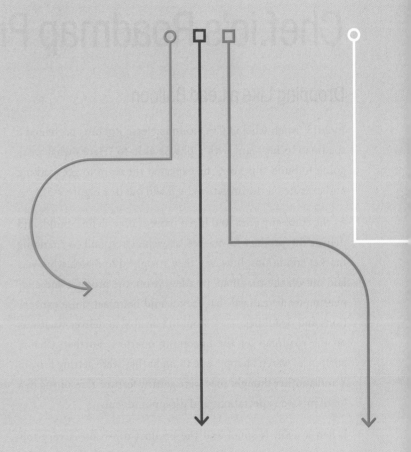

Chef.io's Roadmap Presentation

Dropping Like a Lead Balloon

In 2013, when Chef.io CEO/founder Jesse Robbins presented a roadmap to his team with a phrase akin to "Here's what we're going to build this year," he expected the team to get working and execute on the initiatives he'd laid out (see Figure 9-5).

As the company grew and hired more staff to define, build, and deliver the product to market, as well as respond to changing market conditions, however, they struggled to match what was laid out on the roadmap. In a few years, the product and engineering team realized that they would not meet those expectations and deadlines. They wouldn't be able to deliver what was on the roadmap for the upcoming quarters. Further, Chef.io customers weren't happy: one thought they were getting feature X and another thought they were getting feature Y, resulting in a lot of missed expectations and disappointment.

When a team is small and the product direction is very top-down, this phenomenon is quite common. It makes sense in theory: those who started the company and established the initial product vision lay out the roadmap for the future versions. In practice, though, those now-executive-level CEOs, CTOs, and CPOs have become more removed from the specific details and challenges of the product team, so they overestimate what can be accomplished and by when. The roadmap needs to account for this growth.

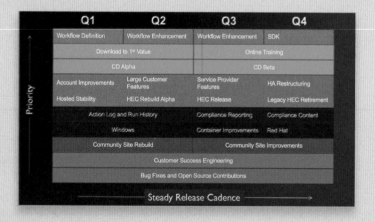

FIGURE 9-6. *Chef.io's 2013 roadmap*

Making Changes

Julian Dunn, the Chef.io product manager, convinced the team to make some changes. Like any smart team, they revised their roadmaps and changed both the internal as well as external versions. Using ProdPad to manage their internal roadmap, they arranged the themes on cards, relating each theme to a business objective, in a Current–Near Term–Future layout (see Figure 9-6). Clicking into the card reveals more detailed information, but the theme level works well for the team. For example, the card that reads Minimum Configuration Installation essentially is a way of asking, "How can we make our products easier for the cloud?" The related objective is to make a more cloud-based product (though, as of this writing, Chef Automate is an on-premise software requiring on-site installation).

To address the customer's missed expectations, the product team turned over the ProdPad-based roadmap to the product marketing team, who pulled information from that to create a slide-based artifact suitable for presentation that offers up some framing of the roadmap to the audience (likely customers and partners).

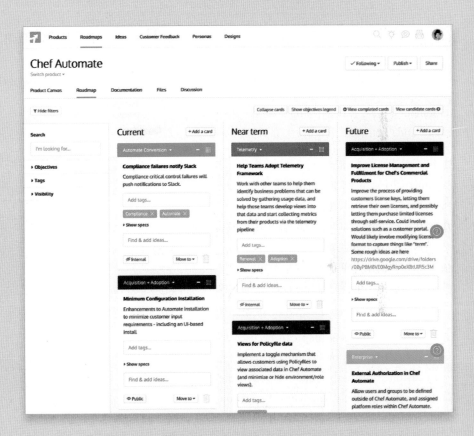

FIGURE 9-7. *Chef.io's revised, theme-based product roadmap*

CASE STUDY: Chef.io's Roadmap Presentation

Slide 1 has an introduction and, more important, qualifiers and a disclaimer (Figure 9-7).

Slide 2 shows some of the metrics and recent progress, as well as defining three product development cycles: "Considering," "In development," and "Released" (Figure 9-8).

Slide 3 then shares information from the Prod-Pad internal roadmap. It collapses some of the "Near term" and "Future" time horizons, and while this exposes features the team is considering, it does not offer too much detail and is framed in a way that avoids a firm commitment on delivering these particular feature sets (Figure 9-9).

This portion of the roadmap can be used to get feedback from customers and prospects. If every customer reacts to a roadmapped theme (or feature!) negatively, the team may reconsider. To reiterate what we've said many times in the book: a roadmap is not a promise or commitment for a set of features.

(Slides 4 and 5 containing features "In development" and "Released" are not shown.)

The Chef Roadmap

Roadmap Inputs
- Direct customer input (feedback.chef.io)
- Market research
- Team experience
- Product performance

Qualifiers
- User & customer value
- Business performance metrics
- Feasibility
- Commitment to win
- One-off features vs. built for market

Proprietary & Confidential

Subject to change at any time

This presentation contains forward looking statements regarding future operations, product development, product capabilities. This information is subject to change at any time without prior notice. Actual results and future plans may differ significantly as a result of, among other things, changes in product strategy. This presentation is not a commitment to deliver any material, code or functionality. Any purchase of software by customers should neither be contingent on the delivery of any future functionality or features, nor dependent on any oral or written public comments made by Chef regarding future functionality or features.

FIGURE 9-8. *Slide 1 of Chef.io's roadmap presentation includes an introduction, qualifiers, and a disclaimer*

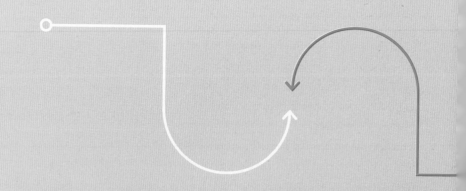

FIGURE 9-9. *Slide 2 shows key metrics, recent progress, and product development cycles*

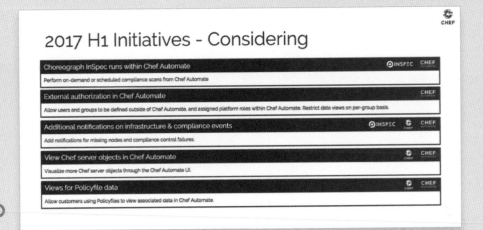

FIGURE 9-10. *Slide 3 shares information from the ProdPad internal roadmap without over-committing or giving too much detail*

Summary

Sharing your roadmap helps obtain buy-in from a variety of stakeholders, even customers. Different stakeholders will look for different information on a product roadmap. A slide-based presentation can help you tell the story of your roadmap clearly and effectively. As with any good presentation, know your audience so you can frame and tailor the content to them, be clear about your goals, and assemble the components of your roadmap to get your key points across and the decisions and/or buy-in you need. A presentation flow that starts with *why*, covers recent progress, and then gets into the *how*, frames up the roadmap details effectively. You're fast on your way to product greatness...until something changes, and of course, things always change.

Chapter 10
Keeping It Fresh

What you'll learn in this chapter

How the roadmap evolves

How far out your roadmap should go

Ways to manage planned change

Ways to manage unplanned change

How to communicate change

Chapter

10

Keeping It Fresh

When conditions in the environment change, your roadmap—like any living thing—must change as well in order to survive.

How would your stakeholders feel if you built what you thought was important nine months ago instead of what is clearly important now?

But wait—your closest competitor just came out with something that's eating into your close rate. And one of your largest customers just announced they won't renew without a feature you ended up cutting. Not only that, but your team tells you that what you had planned for February is going to take until May to deliver.

If only the world would hold still long enough, we could get to the end of our roadmaps, achieve our visions of success, and retire rich and happy. But it never works that way. As we mentioned in Chapter 6, things change, and the closer your product is to the cutting edge, the faster they change. So what do you do?

When conditions in the environment change, your roadmap—like any living thing—must change as well in order to survive. In this chapter, we'll discuss the frequency of change, how to manage it, and how to communicate it.

Roadmap Evolution

Imagine a species of small birds living on the mainland of South America. That species feeds on small, soft seeds common on the continent, and has evolved a small beak that is well adapted for quickly crushing these seeds and swallowing them in quantity. Life is good, and the species multiplies.

Over time, though, the population grows to the point that the supply of these seeds is no longer adequate. Individual birds sometimes have to range far to find enough seeds to survive. Some even fly away from the mainland and happen upon islands where there are no other seed-eating birds to compete with and plenty of seeds for them to feed on and multiply.

The only trouble is that the seeds native to these islands are larger and harder to crush than the seeds on the mainland the birds evolved to eat. It can be a lot of work to get enough nutrition out of these seeds, especially as the population grows and once again is competing for food. In this situation, birds with larger and more powerful beaks have an advantage. They can quickly crush and swallow the native seeds and get more of the available food for themselves than their competitors.

This, so the theory goes, leads to more viable offspring who tend to inherit their parents' larger beaks. And pretty soon, the islands are filled with birds who resemble their mainland cousins in every way except for the size of their beaks.

The sudden change in the food supply forced this species to adapt quickly to their new environment. Having adapted to the island food supply, however, the birds settle into a period of relatively little change. The original birds evolved because of a stimulus, a change in their situation. While the situation remained stable, there was no stimulus to change, and bird beaks remained small.

Evolutionary theory suggests that this is what happened to the Galapagos finches Darwin described in *On the Origin of Species* (see Figure 10-1).

FIGURE 10-1. *The evolution of Galapagos finches*

Given a stable environment, a roadmap should not change either. But most market environments are not completely stable. Technology advances, competitors try to outflank us, fashions wax and wane, customers' wants and needs evolve—even the company mission and strategy may change. Like Darwin's finches, roadmaps are living things and must evolve to fit changes in their environment or face extinction.

Let's look at an example. After executing on a robust roadmap for some months, Gillian Daniel, former VP of Products at smartShift Technologies, saw solid traction on business goals she had set, including increasing revenue per customer. However, she also discovered that margins took a hit as the cost to serve customers rose. This caused the company to reevaluate its objectives, adding "increase profit" (mostly by seeking ways to lower costs) to their prioritization scorecard. As you can imagine, the resulting scoring shifted priorities, and the roadmap was adjusted to fit the new direction, keeping the company in the black while it grew.

This change didn't come on a whim one day, but after analysis of business results, discussion among the executive team, and examination of the implications on commitments already made to customers.

Successful companies revise their roadmaps on a regular cycle to reflect market changes and shifts in strategy or priority, while also allowing execution to proceed steadily between updates. This is similar to the concept of sprints in Agile Scrum development, but on a larger scale. In Scrum, the development team is left alone to execute for a few weeks with no changes in priority. Priorities for the next increment are determined when the output of the first increment is available for analysis.

According to Webster's Collegiate Dictionary, *punctuated equilibrium* is "a theory that evolution proceeds with long periods of relative stability interspersed with rapid change." We believe this is a good metaphor for managing roadmap change in the least disruptive way possible.

That begs the question, however: how stable is your environment? This will determine how far out your roadmap should go, and how frequently you should update it.

How Far Out Should Your Roadmap Go?

The faster the pace of change in your market, the faster your development cycle should be—and the more compressed your roadmap should be in terms of both total timespan and the intervals you choose. While an established product in a mature market that releases new and improved versions once per year will have a correspondingly long roadmap, a startup that is releasing new capabilities every week will have a roadmap that may stretch only a few months into the future.

This is why Intel's public roadmap typically stretches out two to three years (and you can be sure the internal one projects further), as shown in Figure 10-2.

In contrast, many startups favor a simple roadmap format, which uses broader timeframe bucketing like Now, Next, and Later.

Generally, the pace of change and development is directly related to your product's stage of life and the maturity of its market. If companies in your space are still figuring out what the future might hold, it doesn't make sense to spend a lot of time making detailed long-term plans that will surely change.

Use Table 10-1 to help you determine what timeframes are most appropriate for your roadmap based on your product's stage of life.

TABLE 10-1. *Recommended roadmap timeframes based on a product's stage of life*

Product Stage of Life	Timeframe
Discovery	Short (e.g., months)
Growth	Longer (e.g., quarters)
Maturity/decline	Longest (e.g., years)

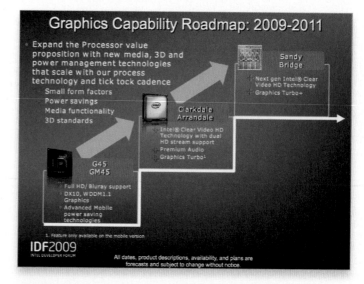

FIGURE 10-2. *This public roadmap from Intel spanned three years*

Planned Change

You might be asking: *But how can I justify changing my road-map partway through? Won't my customers, my partners, my salespeople—my board!—expect me to deliver on my roadmap commitments?*

We're going to go out on a limb and say no. The board and all of these other stakeholders understand and expect you to respond to changes in the market. How would your salespeople feel, as an example, if you stuck to your roadmap but failed to respond to a new competitive threat that was causing them to lose deals? How would your investors feel if you spent their money building what you thought was important nine months ago instead of what is clearly important now?

Even customers understand that your roadmap will evolve over time. (And if they don't, make sure you remind them whenever you discuss the roadmap. See the *Disclaimer* section of Chapter 2 for guidance on forward-looking statements.)

Remember, a roadmap is not a contract. As long as customers see that your essential vision is one they share, considered changes in the path you take to get there are generally OK. When they see clearly that their interests are being served, stakeholders in general are supportive of roadmap changes.

Change Frequency

As we discussed in "How Far Out Should Your Roadmap Go?" organizations in fast-moving industries with rapidly evolving solutions need to update their roadmap at the speed of their business. A rule of thumb is that the refresh rate of your road-map should match the time scale of your roadmap.

If your roadmap is laid out in quarters, you should probably revisit and update it every quarter. Repeating the same steps outlined in this book for creating a new roadmap allows you to regularly reexamine your visions, strategy, goals, and themes to ensure you are still headed along the right path.

Unplanned Change

When Features Are Late

The most common reason for roadmap change is when work is delivered (or it becomes clear it will be delivered) later than planned. In Chapter 6, we talk about how these delays sometimes result in carryover items that get pushed from one roadmap version to the next. In tech companies, product development seems always to be late. Similarly, supply-chain delays always seem to slow manufacturing output.

If you are focused on a certain outcome you want to achieve for your customer and your company, you can absorb changes to the output of your operation and shift your resources to maximize results against those outcomes.

Sometimes, however, delays occur that necessitate reevaluation of your roadmap at a high level. Enter what's called the **iron triangle** (see Figure 10-3).

FIGURE 10-3. *The iron triangle*

Ideally, you'd like to ship everything on *schedule*, on *budget*, and with the full *scope* and *quality* you envisioned at the start. However, when change happens, you have to adjust accordingly. The four levers of the iron triangle are available for you to push or pull when things don't go as planned. Let's look at each in more detail.

Schedule

The most obvious response to something taking longer than planned is to accept the new date and adjust the roadmap accordingly. This is not always the best option, however, especially if a delay will cause you to default on commitments, miss a market window, or fail to comply with regulations.

Therefore, when the schedule shrinks, you may need to consider decreasing scope or increasing resources to assure an expected level of quality.

An unanticipated delay may also be a symptom of trouble with one of the other variables, so it makes sense to have a detailed discussion with your team and evaluate the situation from all angles before committing to adjustments.

Scope

If it is most important to meet the original schedule, you can look at cutting back on some of what you planned to deliver by that date. You can either deliver in stages (some features on the original date, some later) or deliver what you can on time and move on to other priorities after, depending on your product strategy.

Cutting scope might mean removing some features that are not required to solve for a particular theme, reducing capacity or quantity, or constraining options. It turns out, for example, that the reason Henry Ford famously painted all Model Ts black was that the fast-drying paint his team came up with to accelerate manufacturing (and maintain affordable prices) came only in black.

Sometimes, though, scope cannot be cut or has already been reduced to the point where further cutting makes something unusable for its intended audience. Regulatory compliance, for example, is often a binary thing. Either you comply or you do not, and you can't shave a few things to make up time.

Resources

If you can't change schedule and you can't reduce scope, the next option is to add resources, thus probably blowing the original budget for the project and/or starving other priorities. If it's a simple matter of manufacturing capacity, bringing on a second shift or an additional plant may make sense.

In software and other endeavors leveraging small teams of knowledge workers, however, this approach seldom works. As far back as 1975, Frederick Brooks published his now-famous book, *The Mythical Man-Month* (Addison-Wesley), wherein he demonstrates with data and numerous real-world examples that "adding manpower to a late software project makes it later." And studies have since shown that small teams of three to seven people are most effective at delivering on software projects. This effect is thought to result from the increase in communication overhead necessary to coordinate larger groups. This effect is magnified if new people are added late in the project, thus burdening the existing team with getting the new team members up to speed when time is at a premium. (Amazon.com's famous two-pizza rule is an attempt to apply this team-size principle across an entire large organization.)

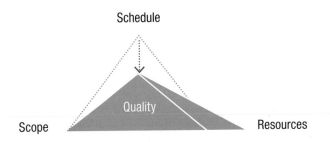

Quality

The less-often-discussed aspect of the iron triangle is quality. When teams attempt to hold all other variables—schedule, scope, and budget—constant despite slippage, quality is what ends up suffering. People work late in an effort to meet unreasonable deadlines and end up making mistakes due to fatigue. Then, as the deadline approaches, they cut corners out of desperation.

As Edward Yourdon explains in his book *Death March* (Prentice Hall), "While the corporate goal of such projects is to overcome impossible odds and achieve miracles, the personal goal of the project manager and team members often shrinks down to mere survival: keeping one's job, maintaining some semblance of a relationship with one's spouse and children, and avoiding a heart attack or ulcer."

This situation can lead to manufacturing defects, software and hardware bugs, and service quality issues that result in poor reviews, product returns, lack of reorder or renewal, and (ironically) delays in future roadmap deliverables because the team is occupied with fixing the quality problems resulting from the compromises made to achieve the prior date.

Software teams sometimes refer to the buildup of quality issues that slow development as *technical debt*, and too much of it can seriously hamper your ability to move your roadmap forward.

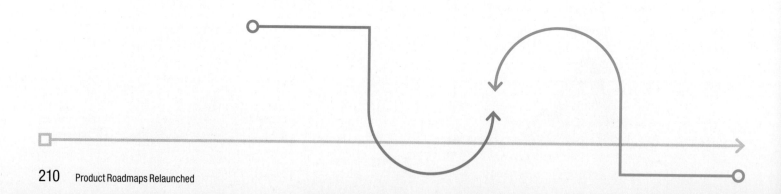

When to Compromise on Quality

Is it ever OK to compromise on quality? Surprisingly, yes.

If you know your product will be used by many millions with minimal changes and refinements over time, it makes sense to invest up front in the kind of foundation that will support that scale. In manufacturing, we develop our tooling for a certain throughput and lifespan based on assumptions about the quantity we will need to produce over a period of time. In software, we plan the database and application layers to handle the expected load of a projected level of simultaneous users. If your quantity of product or number of users is expected to be in the millions, it is necessary to make up-front investments to support that scale. In fact, to skip that investment would be irresponsible. As numbers mounted, you'd be unable to keep up with demand and you might never recover.

But what if your product or service is such a new and untried idea that you cannot make a realistic projection of demand? What if you are so far out on the cutting edge that there is a large chance the initial version of the product will be a flop and you'll have to quickly replace it with something better? What if you might have to iterate several times to arrive at the optimal fit between what your product does and what the market needs?

This is exactly the situation most high-tech startups find themselves in, and exactly the reason why the Lean Startup movement advocates creating *minimum viable products* (MVPs), de-fined in Eric Ries's book *The Lean Startup* (Crown Business) as "that version of a new product which allows a team to collect the maximum amount of validated learning about customers with the least effort."

Ries encourages humility in the service of learning, saying, "Startups that succeed are those that manage to iterate enough times before running out of resources." Working hard to make that first version of your product the best, most scalable, most reusable, most elegantly built thing is likely wasted effort. Worse, it actually slows your progress toward putting something in front of customers that you can learn from and then change based on their feedback. Once you have hit on a success, then it makes sense to go back and rebuild experiment #6 to the quality and scale required.

What combination of the four variables in the iron triangle you decide to play with depends on what is most important to your business. If you have a hard deadline you really can't move without serious consequences to your business, then you're going to have to look at scope, budget, and/or quality. If, on the other hand, scope is paramount, you may want to give on schedule and/or another variable. You can never have everything, but you can pick which goals to focus on and decide where compromise is the least painful.

Special Requests

Another frequent challenge to an established roadmap is the request to "slip in" a feature, fix, or one-off version for a "special" customer or a partner. This often will come from sales. "If we can just add this one little thing," they'll plead, "we can close this big deal and make the quarter."

Whenever a request comes in that, if granted, would adjust the roadmap, we recommend asking three questions:

1. What problem is this request trying to solve?

This question can help you get past the specific request to the real customer need. Very often, sales (or even the procurement department at the company you are selling to) will not actually know why the request is being made. It's important that you, the product person, learn why this request is important (other than that it purportedly will clinch the deal).

We recommend that you try to speak directly to the requestor, and then trace it back to the person with the underlying problem that needs solving. Sit with that person or interview them over the phone and learn about their circumstances. Ask them what they are trying to accomplish and how they imagine fulfilling this request.

You may have to ask why multiple times before you get to the root of the problem. Most often, specific feature requests are one person's guess as to the best solution to an unstated problem.

Learning who that person is allows you to evaluate whether they are in your target market. And learning what that problem really is enables you and your team to generate alternate ways of solving it that may be less disruptive to your roadmap, better for the original requestor, and possibly more applicable to *all* of your customers.

2. Does solving that need align with our objectives?

This question allows you to distinguish between simply providing value and making progress toward the goals you've spent so much effort defining and rallying stakeholders around. If the whole organization is focused on entering a new market, why would you slow progress on that effort by building features for a market that's tapped out?

3. Is it more important than what's on the roadmap now?

This question focuses the discussion on trade-offs. Though stakeholders often conveniently forget this, the iron triangle dictates that adding something in means cutting something out (or delaying it or adding resources). Many times it will not make sense to displace existing roadmap items with a special request, but sometimes it will. See Chapter 7 for some objective ways to evaluate the priority of one feature against others.

As we mentioned in earlier chapters, pet projects from your stakeholders are also a frequent challenge to the plan. Somehow, the individual(s) in question always seems to think that adding more work to an already challenging schedule will inspire the team to greater heights.

However, adding scope will unquestionably have an effect on one or more of the other variables in the iron triangle. If you agree to add that scope, then it's best to decide right away which variables will be compromised to accommodate it. Not choosing is to let chance decide for you.

The easiest thing to do is swap out something already planned, thus managing scope back to its original size and leaving the other variables unaffected. This works well if your roadmap consists of themes only (see Chapter 5). A theme that describes the benefits but leaves out specifics about features gives you flexibility to cut specific features to make room for late-breaking requests.

External Pressures

The reason games like chess are a contest at all is that it's not possible to predict precisely what your opponent will do in the future. Business competitors are the same. You can make a reasonable guess about how they will respond to your moves in the marketplace, but you can never be certain.

Similarly, you cannot predict with accuracy when the economy will rise or fall, when prices will inflate or stagnate, when new regulations will emerge, or when fashions will change (or in what direction). Analysts around the world expend a lot of energy attempting to forecast these things, but even they don't agree. You must make some educated guesses about the future state of the world (or at least your market) in order to set direction, but you must also plan for being wrong.

These unforeseen changes in the market will at some point affect your strategy and therefore your roadmap—and sometimes they won't occur on a nice, neat, quarterly schedule. What's a product person to do? Respond and adjust the roadmap.

You might argue that you have a vision and that you plan to stick to it, come what may. As long as you are still solving a real problem for people who are willing and able to pay, you should stay the course, but you will get there faster and with less risk if you adjust your precise route based on the weather or traffic conditions.

Changes in Strategy

That said, at some point in the life cycle of many businesses, there comes a time when you realize your strategy and your goals are all wrong. At that point, the business may decide to *pivot*—that is, to implement what Eric Ries describes in *The Lean Startup* as "a change in strategy without a change in vision."

For example, in the 1980s Intel was facing increasing price pressure from Japanese manufacturers in their mainstay memory chip business. Andy Grove and his then-CEO Gordon Moore looked at their future in this business, realized how poor their prospects were, and decided to make a strategic move into microprocessors. They completely exited the memory business, refocused their strategy on a better market, and ended up creating one of the most profitable companies in the world.

Intel was even then a large company, but pivoting is much more common in startups. Fred Wilson of Union Square Ventures says that 17 of 26 companies in his portfolio "made complete transformations or partial transformations of their businesses" between investment and exit. That's 65%!

The upshot here is that it doesn't make sense to wait for a regularly scheduled roadmap review to change strategy. When it's time for a pivot, revisit everything from the product vision down, and be explicit about what is changing, what is not changing, and why these changes are necessary.

Communicating Change

Whether it's part of a regularly scheduled roadmap update or in reaction to unanticipated shifts in external forces, when the roadmap changes, it is critical to the success of your efforts that you clearly and broadly communicate the *why*, *what*, and *when* of roadmap updates. Everyone needs the latest version of the treasure map if you are all going to dig in the same spot, right?

Why

The reasons change is occurring may be the most important part of a roadmap update, and yet this information is often left out. People are often embarrassed about the necessity for change, and they want to avoid scrutiny or argument about it. But leaving your team without a clear reason why is worse—it can undermine their confidence in the strategy and the leadership and invite them to make up their own (less-than-charitable) reasons.

Don't shy away from discussing change. Embrace it and get everyone on board. We recommend socializing changes just the way you would socialize a new roadmap created from scratch (see Chapter 8 if you need a refresher).

Regardless of the impetus to change, the focus of your discussion must be on how, given the new reality, the changes in the roadmap will result in a better future for the company, the customer, and all of the stakeholders.

This is easy if you refer back to the vision, strategy, and goals you developed for the original (or most recent) roadmap. In most cases, your vision won't have changed. Your strategy will often be unchanged as well. However, one of your goals may have been achieved, may have proven to be too ambitious, or may simply no longer be as relevant.

Suppose your goal of entering a new market has been achieved. You've signed on 100 customers, your close rate is pretty good, and you are collecting feedback from those new customers that there are some missing capabilities they really expect and need. It would probably make sense at this stage to replace your goal of entering that market with one of growing your business there, or possibly of increasing your renewal or reorder rate. This change would in turn likely refocus your roadmap on delivering those missing capabilities. Is this a bad change? No, it's an indication of progress. Celebrate it!

Suppose, conversely, that your goal of penetrating this new market has manifestly *not* been achieved. Perhaps you've been able to sell only a few units, and those customers do not seem happy. Maybe your analysis shows there are cheaper alternatives with greater capabilities. You tested the waters and found them turbulent. What's your next move?

That depends on your vision and your strategy. If this market is a key part of your vision and your first forays have identified some new themes that are the keys to success, then you should probably add those themes to your roadmap. If, like Intel's Andy Grove, however, you realize that your strategy is likely to fail in this market, it's time to pivot to a new strategy for achieving your vision. Perhaps there is a more attractive adjacent market, or a narrow slice of this new market that is willing to pay more for your unique solution.

You have limited resources; if you determine this is not the best use of your team's time and effort, redirect them where they will be most successful. Giving your team the context for a change will inspire them to move forward with it instead of clinging to the old strategy.

What and When

If you've done a good job of setting the stage for change, your stakeholders will be hungry for the specifics. They will want to know how any shift in strategy or priorities affects the expectations you've set for deliverables.

Changes might be *small*—for example, adding or dropping a single subtheme for the next release or version, or changing a date by a week. This type of change may not necessarily affect your roadmap. They may affect the release or project plan, however.

Changes might be *broad-reaching*—for example, moving a theme planned for next year forward many months to be the next big focus, or dropping a theme that no longer seems crucial to success.

Changes can also be *fundamental*—as when the company or product pivots to a completely new strategy. In such cases, the themes, subthemes, and features of a roadmap may be changed or replaced entirely.

For the broad-reaching and fundamental changes, you'll need to update your roadmap, inform all your stakeholders, and obtain buy-in—and if you've read this far, you know what all of that entails.

Roadmap Changes

If a roadmap is in some ways a story about how you envision success for your stakeholders such as the broad-reaching or fundamental levels, a roadmap update must tell the story of how you learned something that caused you to change direction.

Suppose it's been nearly six months since this roadmap was created, and circumstances have changed a bit. Development and manufacturing of the indestructible Wombat hose is on schedule, but apparently, there have been difficulties with leaks in the 40-foot version.

Let's revisit the current roadmap of our fictitious garden hose company. It consisted of these primary components:

- Product Vision: To perfect American lawns and landscapes by perfecting water delivery

- Business Objectives: 1M unit sales, <5% returns, <2% defects, Double average selling price (ASP)

- Timeframes: H1 2017, H2 2017, 2018, and 2019

- Themes: Roadmap to Perfecting Water Delivery, consisting of seven themes delivered over three years, and three features supporting the first theme to be delivered in the next six months

- Disclaimer

After much analysis of the market, your take is that the "no-leak connections" claim is more important than having a second, longer model. You have decided, therefore, to ship only the 20-foot model for now and delay the longer model until the "extended reach" theme planned for the following year (when you plan also to develop an 80-foot model).

This change at the feature level, though, is nothing compared to the strategic opportunity you've identified in fertilizer. A few of your early test customers have discovered that your hoses are much better than most at delivering fertilizer. Apparently the Wombat hoses' more rugged construction keeps them from clogging like cheaper hoses often do when spraying dissolved solids. Your research uncovers widespread dissatisfaction with the performance of competitors in this area and pent-up demand for an effective solution.

Suddenly, something you had planned as a theme a couple of years out looks more like something that will provide clear differentiation in your target market. You do your market research and your business projections. You discuss timelines with your development team and manufacturing partners. You shuttle between stakeholders and socialize the opportunity as well as its significance in terms of roadmap changes. You even go to the board and preview a possible change to your stated strategy.

In the end, you decide to move "Fertilizer Delivery" up from 2019 to the second half of 2017. You also reach agreement with the board that if you meet certain thresholds in sales, you will adjust your *product vision* to read, "To perfect the landscapes of affluent Americans by perfecting *nutrient* delivery," and develop new themes along these lines.

Figures 10-4 through 10-9 show what your slides might look like at a quarterly roadmap review with the executive team or the board (see Chapter 9 for a reminder on detailed recommendations for presenting the roadmap).

FIGURE 10-4.

Remind your audience that your company vision hasn't changed by showing the same slide you showed a quarter before

Perfecting Water Delivery

H1'17	H2'17	2018	2019
Indestructible hose	Fertilizer Delivery	Putting Green Evenness for Lawns	Infinite Extensibility
40' Length No-leak connections No-kink armor In stores May 1	Severe Weather Handling	Extended Reach 80' Length	Delicate Flower Management

Updated March, 2017

FIGURE 10-7.

Show the updated version of the roadmap without the markup; this is the new version you will share outside the review meeting (note the date in the lower-left corner)

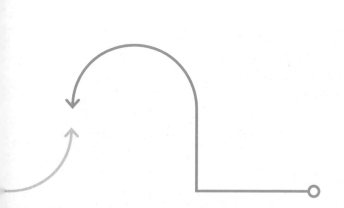

FIGURE 10-5.

Describe the opportunity to enter the fertilizer delivery business and provide the rationale for the change, explaining why it benefits both the customer and the company

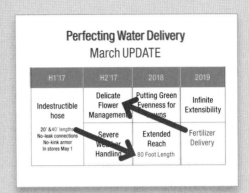

FIGURE 10-6.

Visually indicate which themes and which specific features are changing or moving on the roadmap with colors, arrows, pop-ups, or whatever is necessary to annotate your roadmap clearly

FIGURE 10-8.

Make the newly accelerated item on the roadmap real with a diagram, photo, or mockup

FIGURE 10-9.

Preview the new strategy that will go into effect if your fertilizer theme is successful—you will likely not share this outside of the roadmap review with executives unless it takes hold

Forks in the Road

The situation of our fictitious garden hose company is not that unique, actually. Many companies (especially startups) face strategic forks in the road, where they must answer questions like these:

Do we grow revenue by going down market to a larger number of smaller customers, or do we differentiate further to support higher prices among our high-end customers?

Do we pursue a promising but untried technology, or do we focus on unit cost reduction?

Do we focus on channel partners, or sell direct?

Rather than pursue all avenues at once, successful organizations often focus on one opportunity at a time, but leave the door open to pivot or expand in the future if the situation warrants.

Having played multiple scenarios out on paper, the garden hose company has concluded one option is the best, and its roadmap reflects this decision. There are always risks, however, and one or a few other options may have been almost as attractive.

One way to disentangle this situation is to test the underlying assumptions in your projections. If path #1 is the correct one, you should see signs of success at some point along that path. And if you can incorporate thresholds (reference Chapter 4's discussion about key results)—specific performance numbers your product needs to achieve—into your roadmap, you can build optionality and decision criteria right into your plan.

Our garden hose company might, for example, build a roadmap with one pathway that assumes delivery of fertilizer is a huge winner for the company, and another pathway that assumes it is but one among many themes built around specialized needs (Figure 10-10). Which path is ultimately followed depends on the performance of the initial product for fertilizer delivery.

This decision will have such profound effects on the company direction that, in addition to the roadmap visualization itself, it requires additional information on the decision criteria (Figure 10-11). If you were to travel from point A to point B and decided that a ferry was how you'll get there, you couldn't suddenly, in the middle of the ferry trip, decide that you want to take a car instead. You'll have to finish the ferry trip and then get into a car, so this type of information gives a team foresight into how to plan out their future product, which can have impact on how the near-term development is done.

This additional information may be presented at a stakeholder buy-in meeting (see Chapter 8 for buy-in meetings and Chapter 9 for presenting and sharing).

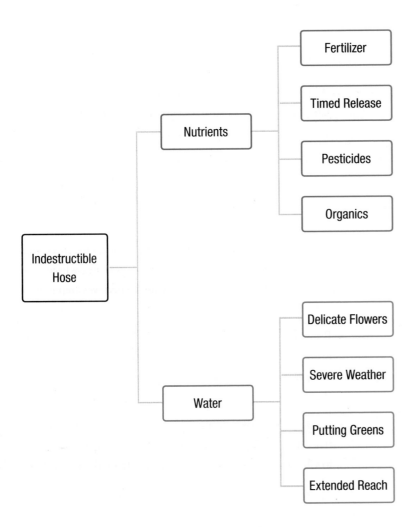

FIGURE 10-10. *Which path our garden hose company ultimately follows depends on the performance of our initial product for fertilizer delivery*

Nutrient Strategy Decision

If fertilizer delivery is to become a core part of our strategy, it must:

- Be #1 or #2 reason for purchase >50%

- Exceed Q4 sales projections for severe weather version by 50%

- Bake off campaign rated at least 4/5 for persuasiveness

FIGURE 10-11. *The decision criteria behind the proposed new business objectives*

Lather, Rinse, Repeat

Whatever process you follow to create your first roadmap, you will have to revisit it at intervals that match the pace of change in your market.

How deep you will need to go on subsequent revisions, however, depends on how much things have changed since the last version.

- Whenever you revisit your roadmap, we suggest you review Chapter 8 to help ensure the buy-in is smooth and transparent. This may be sufficient if changes are minor.

- If your product vision has not changed, but you have new priorities based on changes in your market, we suggest you review Chapter 7 to ensure these changes have a clear rationale.

- If you have made such progress on solving customer and organizational needs that you are moving into whole new areas of functionality, you may want to review Chapter 6 to ensure you are focused on providing real value.

- If customer or organizational needs have changed, or you are serving new types of customers, you may want to review Chapter 5 to ensure you've identified the most important themes to focus on.

- If your company's vision, strategy, or key business objectives have changed, you may want to go all the way back to Chapter 3 to rethink your roadmap from the ground up.

As you can see, the deeper the changes, the further back in this book you may need to go!

Evolve.

Summary

No plan survives first contact with the enemy.

—Attributed to Prussian Field Marshal
Helmuth von Moltke the Elder

No matter how well you plan, change is unavoidable. Following the steps in this book won't help you develop a plan that's immune to change, but it *will* help you create one that can evolve with it.

Have a regular process for reassessing your roadmap and communicating the why, what, and when of any changes you make.

When change is necessary (and leading up to your regular roadmap updates), assess the depth of that change and decide how far back you need to go in the process described in this book to revisit assumptions.

In the final chapter, we'll recap what you've learned throughout the book and offer some tips on where to go from here.

Relaunching Roadmaps in Your Organization

What you'll learn in this chapter

How to assess your organization's "roadmap health"

Whether to course-correct or have a full relaunch

Chapter

11

Relaunching Roadmaps in Your Organization

If you've read through this whole book, it's probably because, like many other product people, you've grown frustrated with the traditional roadmapping process.

ikely your organization is either bogged down in a futile effort to predict the unpredictable, or your team has given up on roadmaps and is operating sprint to sprint or customer demand to customer demand.

If you've read this far, though, you know a roadmap can be so much more than a doomed wish list of features and dates. You've seen the examples of how companies like Slack, Contactually, Tesla, and Chef communicate their product vision and show clearly how they will achieve it and their business objectives by solving market problems.

Throughout this book, we've tried to show you how organizations like these use roadmaps to:

- Put the organization's plans in a strategic context
- Focus on delivering value to customers and the organization
- Embrace learning as part of a successful product development process
- Rally the organization around a single set of priorities
- Get customers excited about the product's direction

At the same time, we've tried to show how these organizations avoid:

- Making promises product teams aren't confident they will deliver on
- A wasteful process of up-front design and estimation
- Conflating a roadmap with a project plan or a release plan

How to Get Started

We suggest *a six-step process* for getting started in your organization:

1. Assess your situation and choose an approach.

2. Get buy-in for change from from your key stakeholders.

3. Train your stakeholders how to contribute.

4. Start small and work incrementally.

5. Evaluate your results and align on next steps.

6. Keep relaunching.

Step 1. Assess your situation

Before you can propose a solution, you need to define the problem. (Sound familiar?) It's the same with organizational change. Before you can decide where to begin with a roadmap relaunch, you need to assess your current process (or decide if there even is one).

We suggest you begin by answering the 14 questions in this checklist (Table 11-1). If you are unsure of the criteria, refer to the chapter indicated.

The maximum possible score is 22. If your score is 18 or higher, congratulations, you have a great roadmapping process. Use Approach A described on page 232 to tweak and enhance your already stellar process. If you score a 12 or higher, you're still in reasonably good shape. You should also take Approach A, but recognize that you have a lot of improvements to make and it will take some time to achieve a world-class process. If you've scored 11 or lower, you either have no process or things are so broken currently that you need to set an entirely new baseline. If that's your situation, jump to Approach B.

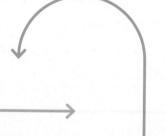

Roadmap Health Assessment Checklist

0–2 scale
0 = entirely or mostly no
1 = sort of maybe, not sure
2 = definitely yes

TABLE 11-1. *Answering and scoring these questions will help you determine how to begin your roadmap relaunch*

		Score
Strategic context	Do you have a clear product vision that most stakeholders can explain? (Chapter 4)	+
	Do you have measurable business objectives that most stakeholders are aware of? (Chapter 4)	+
Focus on value	Does your roadmap focus on customer needs? (Chapter 5)	+
	Are all of the things on the roadmap clearly tied to customer needs and/or business objectives? (Chapter 2)	+
Embrace learning	Do you update your roadmap regularly, leveraging an evolving process? (Chapter 10)	+
	Do you allow time in the roadmap to learn whether solutions are working before committing to solving a customer need? (Chapter 2)	+
Rally the organization around priorities	Do you use an objective and accepted method of prioritization? (Chapter 7)	+
	Do you have an established process for achieving alignment with stakeholders? (Chapter 8)	+
	Do you regularly present and share your roadmap with key stakeholders? (Chapter 9)	+
Get customers excited	Do you regularly present and share your roadmap with customers? (Chapter 9)	+
	Do you seek customer feedback on the roadmap and incorporate it in your process? (Chapter 8)	+
Avoid overpromising*	Do you have specific features, solutions, fixes, or other deliverables on your roadmap? (Chapter 6)	-
	Do you have precise or "best-case" dates for things on your roadmap? (Chapter 9)	-
Avoid overdesigning and overplanning*	Do you throughly design a solution before putting a customer need or problem on the roadmap? (Chapter 5)	-
	Do you have project info like resources, milestones, and dependencies embedded in the roadmap? (Chapter 9)	-

Subtract from score

Total:

Approach A: Course Corrections

If you have a pretty good process and you feel it could be enhanced, you're in a good position. Use the preceding questions to identify the most promising opportunities for improvement, prioritize those using one of the methods we describe in Chapter 7 (critical path would be good here), and focus on improving one part of the process at a time.

If your process is really not working for you but you think it is salvageable with some work, the approach is the same. Don't try to fix everything at once. Use the preceding questions to identify the missing or most-broken parts of your process, prioritize these, and focus on one at a time. It's tempting to change many things at once, but if you've got something that's basically functional, you'll make quicker progress with a single focus.

Approach B: The Full Relaunch

If you don't currently have a process you can salvage and improve upon, it's time to establish one. In this situation, we recommend beginning at the beginning and following the steps described in this book in order, beginning with Chapter 3 on gathering inputs and following through to Chapter 10 on keeping it fresh.

This can be overwhelming, however, and even experienced teams can take months to arrive at a product roadmap and an update process they are happy with. One way we've found very effective to relaunch your roadmapping process is to hold a roadmap workshop. Very much like a Design Sprint, a roadmap workshop brings together the key stakeholders from around your organization in a collaborative effort to define a product vision, objectives, customer needs, and other aspects of a roadmap. We can highly recommend *Design Sprint* from O'Reilly, coauthored by our very own C. Todd Lombardo! They do this in a focused period of time, usually over a few days, to create an initial version of the product roadmap and agree on next steps such as customer validation and a cadence for revision.

An expert facilitator can be very useful in a cross-functional effort such as this because they are completely unbiased toward any particular department or function. They should also bring an established framework, and experience from a variety of previous engagements. If you've read this book, however, you may be the best expert in your organization!

Step 2. Get buy-in for change from from your key stakeholders

Whether you decide to improve an existing process or start fresh, you will be making change. Like a good roadmap, change requires alignment among the people involved. You can't just change the process by fiat and expect people who work in other departments to go along without question. Review Chapter 8 on buy-in and alignment for techniques like shuttle diplomacy and co-creation workshops to identify and then fold your stakeholders into the process of change.

Then feel free to share the results of your Roadmap Health Assessment from the preceding checklist—even better, involve your stakeholders in the assessment by asking everyone to go through the questions on their own and then comparing answers.

Remember that you are seeking alignment, not necessarily consensus, They may not all agree on how broken the process is or which areas need the most focus. That's OK. If you can get them to agree on the necessity for change, it will be easier to get them to give you some leeway on how to approach it.

Step 3. Train your stakeholders how to contribute

Remember also that this is a new approach for many people used to traditional roadmapping. Knowing your audience—that they will likely come with expectations for feature and date commitments, for example—will help you explain what's different about roadmapping this time, why, and how it will be better.

As we discussed in Chapter 8, product roadmapping is not a solo pursuit. Every stakeholder has a part to play and an obligation to contribute. Often times, they just need to be shown how.

Feel free to borrow from this book, both the principles for relaunching roadmaps recapped previously and the steps in the roadmapping process outlined in the various chapters. To help with all of this, we've posted a slide deck with everything you'll need to prepare the launchpad for your roadmap relaunch at *www.productroadmapping.com*.

Step 4. Start small and work incrementally

Look for every opportunity to start small and demonstrate early success. If you're using approach A to course-correct an existing process, this will be natural. Pick the portion of the process you want to focus on and align with your stakeholders on what an improvement looks like. Set a goal you can achieve in a few weeks, like incorporating one of the prioritization models from Chapter 7 or defining some short-term business objectives. Even a small success will allow you to quickly gather support for further improvements.

Even if you are relaunching your roadmapping process entirely as we describe in approach B, you can limit the scope of the effort in other ways. A roadmapping workshop is comprehensive, but takes only a few days to execute, for example. You can also limit involvement in your relaunched roadmap until you gain some confidence in the results. You might, for instance, include only the product core described in Chapter 3: the product people, engineers, and designers most closely involved in your product effort. You can then slowly expand the circle of stakeholders you share the roadmap with, evaluating feedback after every encounter.

Step 5. Evaluate your results and align on next steps

Many product teams have a period of evaluation after they release a product or a feature to market. Sometimes called a *discovery* period, this is when they learn whether the thing they released has had the effect they wanted for customers and for the organization. This is good practice for internal changes like these as well. While you may not need to set formal business objectives for changes you make to the roadmapping process, it's smart to gather your stakeholders periodically, review the changes you've made, and seek feedback on the effects—intended or not—they have had. This will allow you to align on whether to stay the course, change course and try again, or head back to base to try a different direction.

If you have a cross-functional product steering committee, you can use these regular meetings to review your progress and align on next steps. If not, perhaps establishing a regular meeting is a good idea anyway. This same team can be leveraged to review actual product results and inform roadmap planning. Your needs may vary, but many such teams meet every three to six weeks. More often is seldom productive as there hasn't been enough time for the results of change to be felt. Less often frequently prevents the team from gelling, and shared context is quickly lost.

Make sure your team knows you intend to continue to evolve the process. Your team should help you identify where and how the process can be improved over time. Hitting roadblocks or detouring around dysfunctions is natural and to be expected. The key is to acknowledge that the ecosystem is dynamic, and then have the confidence to roll with it and learn.

Step 6. Keep relaunching

It's important to recognize that change is hard for many people—and especially so for organizations. Worse yet, it's hardest when crossing organizational boundaries. You will likely face resistance to change from people within your organization (even your own team) who don't perceive the necessity for change, or who feel threatened by change, or who simply have other priorities. Don't give up. We've seen positive changes at large and small product organizations all over the world.

Gillian's Story of Roadmap Change

From 2014 until mid-2016, Gillian Daniel headed product at smartShift Technologies. Her objective was to get the company into a controlled and predictable growth mode, which required redefining their solutions (bundles of technology and services), as well as positioning and messaging. They also created two new add-on products.

To set the stage for this change, Gillian worked with the executive team to define a vision for what the company wanted to be, what problem they wanted to solve in the world, and for whom.

With a clear vision in place, she was able to propose specific business objectives—outcomes the company was looking for from its product development efforts—including revenue per customer, and penetration into new markets. These goals then became the yardstick against which all proposed new products or product enhancements were judged.

To manage this process, Gillian developed a scorecard that ranked each idea against each of the company's business objectives on a simple high-medium-low scale. She then asked Engineering for a quick T-shirt sizing of each idea. The ideas that got the highest rating on multiple goals for the least effort were the ones that were considered for development.

This scorecard wasn't the final approval for projects, however. Gillian feels strongly that gaining alignment among the key stakeholders in management on a plan is far more important than any particular feature or new product idea. If the team is all pulling together in one direction, they will move faster and be more successful.

So she used this scorecard as a framework to support one-on-one discussions with the executives about priorities, playing out various scenarios, and arriving at a plan through what we call **shuttle diplomacy.**

Each of Gillian's product managers was responsible for publishing a roadmap for their product or product line. These focused heavily on the strategy—the "why" of what was proposed—much more than the details of the planned features. "That context is necessary," explains Gillian, "to make sure each team member is armed with the right information to make all of the day-to-day decisions that pop up in their respective jobs. Without that, they deliver the wrong things because the plan—or tactics—to execute on the strategy can never be perfectly thought out."

After executing on these plans for some months, the company made solid progress on revenue per customer, validating Gillian's approach. However, margins took a hit as the cost to serve customers rose. This caused Gillian and team to reevaluate their goals, adding profit (mostly via seeking ways to lower costs) to the scorecard. The resulting scoring shifted priorities, and the roadmap was adjusted to fit the new direction with little fuss. The company bounced back to profitable growth, significantly increasing its US customer base and revenue to complement the existing European business.

Stories like Gillian's are inspiring. Remember, though, that it's not all going to happen at once. And you're not going to get it all right on the first try. Every launch is eventually followed by a relaunch. We wish we could provide a one-size-fits-all road-mapping template, but the reality is your roadmap has to fit your product and your organization. Any attempt to force-fit a cookie-cutter powerpoint template or project plan will fail, but bringing your stakeholders through an incremental process like the one we outline here is something we've each seen work consistently.

Postscript

We hope the framework, techniques, and examples we've described in this book have been both inspiring and useful for you—not just in relaunching product roadmaps at your organization, but in successfully achieving your vision of a world that's better with your product in it. Check out the love letters some of our roadmap workshop participants have written to their relaunched roadmapping processes.

However, don't stop there. Find ways to share your learning. In return, this will help you learn from others; the best way to get help is to offer it first. We encourage you to talk regularly with other product professionals. Find out how your counterparts in other organizations run their product teams and roadmap-ping process. What kinds of dysfunctions or roadblocks have they encountered? How did they address or resolve them? What does their roadmap look like, and how does it differ from yours? What does a day in the life look like for them? Who are their stakeholders, and how are decisions made? Putting yourself out there will encourage others to do the same, and this level of collaboration within the world of product management will help us all grow and improve.

One last recommendation: look outside your market or industry. Get out of your comfort zone so you can expand your perspective. If you're building a digital product, connect with product people working on physical products or building service-based businesses. Or if you're working on a B2C product, reach out to your peers in the B2B space to see how they operate. Take time to understand how their situations affect their roadmap components and processes. What are they doing effectively that you might be able to adopt?

Like yours, our process of learning never stops. We've set up *www.productroadmapping.com* as a place where we can continue to share what we learn over time about product roadmapping. If you have questions, challenges, ideas, stories, tools, or for that matter, roadmaps you want to share, we hope you'll drop by and continue learning with us.

—*Bruce, C. Todd, Evan, and Michael*

Liftoff.

DEAR ROADMAP,

I AM SO EXCITED TO BE GOING ON THIS JOURNEY WITH YOU!

I HOPE TOGETHER WE CAN:

1) FOCUS ON WHAT PEGA DOES WELL

2) IMPROVE THE USER EXP WITH REAL USERS IN MIND

3) STRENGHEN OUR OFFERINGS WITH AI

I KNOW TOGETHER WE CAN DO GREAT THINGS!

- JAMIE

Dear Roadmap, ♡

I look across the room and my heart fills with glee. Your roadmap gives you a sense of direction and you know where you want to be.

I yearn for what you have, you can give me so much more then I have now.

Give me some of your time, let me feel the emotion of achievement. You can fill the void I have in my life.

DON'T IGNORE ME ANYMORE!

x ♡ YOUR SECRET ADMIRER.

Dear Roadmap,

I wish I had you in my life. The guidance and direction you provide is something I long for here at Pega. My designs would be so much better if only I knew what I was designing for. My design process would be more efficient if I knew when things were needed ahead of time. I hope I find you someday.

— Chris

Dear Roadmap,

It would be so awesome if we had you. We could understand what we needed to do in the short term, and long term, and we could have actual designs ready for team (instead of the giant mess we have today!)

The entire company would understand why we do the things we do, and when we should do them. We'd even be able to understand how much it should all cost.

Wouldn't it be great?

If we only had you, roadmap...

Sincerely,
Stan

Dear Roadmap...

How do I love thee? Let me count the ways:

1) You are an extension of a visual representation of how we intend to achieve our product vision

2) You clearly demonstrate valuable problems to solve

3) You inform the organization about what the product team is actively working on

4) You enable the launch/readiness planning for stakeholders and teams.

5) You align product/engineering/design around the path forward.

Index

Lynda.com website, 58–59

M

Macanufo, James, 168
Mansour, John, 12
Mapping Experiences (Kalbach), 91–92
market opportunity (financial information),
190–191
Maurya, Ash, 56
McCarthy, Bruce
    on customer roadmap needs, 192
    on prioritizing, 128–129
    on ROI scorecards, 143
    on sales and marketing roadmap needs,
        186
    on shuttle diplomacy, 161
    on themes, 89
meetings and workshops
    about, 167
    co-creation workshops, 167–169
    presenting recommendations, 166
me-too features (prioritization pitfall), 135
metrics and key results, 78–79
Meyers, Carol, 17, 134
Microsoft (company), 7, 73
Mills-Scofield, Deb, 80
minimum to ship features, 150
minimum viable products (MVPs), 136, 212
mission statement
    benefits of, 67
    examples of, 68
    key elements to, 67
Moltke the Elder, Helmuth von, 158
Moore, Gordon, 215
MoSCoW method, 150, 153
Motorola (company), 7

multiple roadmaps, 179
Musk, Elon, 82–83, 103
Must-haves (MoSCoW method), 150
The Mythical Man-Month (Brooks), 210

N

net promotor score, 79
new product phase (product life cycle),
    53–54
Nintendo (company), 80
nonfunctional (engineering-focused) needs,
    95

O

objectives, business. *See* business objectives
Office 365 software, 49
OKRs (objectives and key results), 74–76, 78
On the Origin of Species (Darwin), 205
opportunity costs, 129–130
options (GROW acronym), 163–164
Oracle (company), 7
organizations
    company vision, 68
    delivering value to, 8, 12–13
    duality of benefits for customers and,
        72–73
    guiding principles for, 67–69
    rallying around priorities, 8, 16–17, 229
    relaunching roadmaps in, 228–236
    strategic context for plans, 8, 10–11, 229
Osterwalder, Alex, 56
outcomes
    company vision as, 68
    defining, 57, 80
    outputs versus, 15, 21, 31, 74, 80

themes based on desired, 70, 100
outputs
    defining, 80
    outcomes versus, 15, 21, 31, 74, 80
    themes and, 100
overpromising and underdelivering
    to customers, 9, 20, 229
    risks of sharing roadmaps, 177
    to stakeholders, 9, 20, 229
Oxfam (company), 68

P

pain points, 91, 136–137
perception, Kano model on, 140
personas, 60
planned change, 208
platform considerations (roadmap compo-
        nent)
    defined, 40
    development team needs, 183
plausibility (mission statement), 67
Plush Life example, 149
Poepsel, Matt, 11, 14–15
popularity (prioritization pitfall), 134
Predictive Index (company), 119
presenting and sharing roadmaps
    Chef.io case study, 196–199
    to customers, 192
    to development team, 181–185
    to executives, 190–191
    preparation checklist, 194
    risks of sharing, 177–179
    to sales and marketing teams, 186–188
    sharing internally, 175
    to stakeholders, 180
    suggested sequence for, 195